AC/DC

'Hell Ain't No Bad Place To Be!' by Richard Bunton

Omnibus Press /Savoy Editions

Cover design: Pearce Marchbank
Book design: Stuart Watson
Picture research: Savoy Editions
Typeset by: Steve Rothwells

ISBN 0.7119.0082.5
UK Order No. OP 41771
Printed and bound in Great Britain by
William Clowes Limited, Beccles and London

Exclusive distributors:
Book Sales Limited, 8/9 Frith Street, London W1V 5TZ, England
Music Sales Pty. Limited, 120 Rothschild Avenue, Rosebery, NSW 2018, Australia

Published 1982 by Omnibus Press
(a division of Book Sales Ltd)

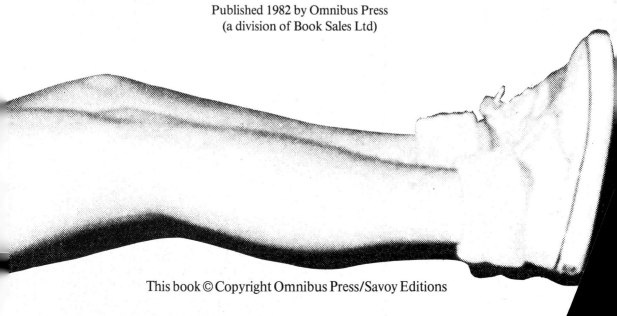

Dedication

To MICHAEL MOORCOCK, whose Condition of Muzak and other Jerry Cornelius novels offer a
credible synthesis of Rock'n'Roll and fiction,

&

LINDA STEELE for her appreciation of the form. And to them both for the hospitality they supplied
during the production of this book.

Acknowledgements are due to Anne Jones for her article Oz Rock (N.M.E., Dec. 1979), Patsy and
Sharon of WEA Records, Thomas Sheridan, John Mottershead, J Jeff Jones and Malcolm Whitehead.
Particular thanks go to Robert Holland for his encyclopedic knowledge of the schoolboy mythos essential
for the analysis in Chapter Two.

Special thanks are due to Stuart Gibbon and Stuart Hutchinson of Newcastle for all their help.
Grateful acknowledgement is also made to the following journals, corporations and individuals for the
reproduction of photographs used in the preparation of this book—Sounds, New Musical Express,
Melody Maker, Fury, Kerrang!, Cream, Trouser Press, WEA records, Atlantic Records, Dick Barnatt,
Yves Coatsaliou, Michael N Marks, Jim Matusik, Kris Guidio, Paul Slattery,
Andrew Darlington, Chris Walter, Charles Partington, Denis O'Regan, Chris Horler, Ross Halfin,
J. Jeff Jones, Andre Csillag and Karl Glauger.

Rock'n'Roll is volcanic. The Earth pours out molten lava. Human beings pour out Rock'n'Roll. For a select minority, that's what life's all about (bet you never got taught *that* at school).

Angus and Malc Young want to *Rock*—and they wanted to let the whole world know it. But all they ever got at school, when they first started, was into fights. They got into fights because the whole authoritarian system for human beings on our planet *stinks.* It puts the lid on Rock'n'Roll. Malc and Angus, like all other Rockers, wanted to *let Rock'n'Roll out of the tin.*

When it was time to leave that blood bath Angus decided to *keep his uniform on.* That way he could show what it was like to let a schoolboy pour out Rock'n'Roll. He could show the world that it was okay for schoolboys everywhere, all around the world, to whip up this shit—yeah, even big 'schoolboys' who had grown up all compressed and outa shape 'cause they'd not had their dials properly attuned. Angus wanted to show forever what it was like to be a schoolboy in this stupid, dangerous, outa-sync planet.

AC/DC

"*I* had drive. I wanted to do it and I knew I'd do it. I just wanted people to sit up and take notice of me. The CHALLENGE. I never mellowed. I never changed. I just stuck at it.

"I was an unhappy schoolboy. Always played truant. I was a bad pupil and only really liked art because you could do what you liked. I once made a six foot long fly out of papier mâché which scared the shit out of everyone on the bus home. My school was the third worst in the state. Many of the kids ended up in reform schools. It was so military. They seemed to take great pride out of keeping you in the dark. They didn't seem to want you to know what was going on in the rest of the world. I was really surprised at the way people lived outside Australia when I left it. People were getting away with a lot more than I ever did."

AC/DC's lead guitarist was born on 31 March, 1959, in overcrowded Glasgow, Scotland. Australia, mostly a vast, four million square miles of desert, and short on numbers, lay like a great vacuum in wait for him. It was popular 20 years ago for post-war European families to try their chances 'Downunder'—and indeed, materialistically, in the areas of this isolated continent where it was possible to work, those with initiative were rewarded. But it is debatable whether young bloods with artistic temperaments would be able to support, or be supported by, such a claustrophobic, frontier atmosphere.

The Youngs, with one daughter and six sons, emigrated to Sydney, Australia, in 1963. Early schooldays in Australia must have been all right for Angus Young, but by the time he reached highschool he found teachers ready to make an example of him, just because of his family home. Elder brother Malcolm had queered his pitch.

Music ran in the blood of the brothers.

"While I was still a little kid in Glasgow, Malcolm was always getting into schoolyard fights. I remember that he got into a lot of trouble with the teachers. He wasn't very popular with some parents either. When I got to Australia his reputation was there ahead of me, so I was caned the first day just to make sure I didn't get any of his ideas."

By the time he was 15 he was given the option to leave or be thrown out. He left. Fortunately for him there was Rock music to fall back on. Music ran in the blood of the brothers. As well as Angus and Malcolm, there were two older brothers, John and George—the former a big guitar influence on Malcolm, and the latter a founding member of the 60s Oz pop band, the Easybeats. The Easybeats had an impact outside Australia. In the mid-60s in Britain they became well known for their chart success, *Friday On My Mind,* which reached No.6, and has since been recorded by other artists, among them David Bowie. Another innovation of George Young's was the production team, Vanda & Young, a partnership formed with co-founder Harry Vanda. Vanda was the lead guitarist of the Easybeats (George was second), and both he and George were the group's writers. The two brothers reappeared in the early 70s with the less successful Marcus-Hook Roll Band, then returned to Oz to get more deeply into production.

life in a confined cage

As producers the two had a tremendous influence on Angus and Malcolm, eventually providing a ready-made, highly sympathetic production unit for AC/DC. The first four AC/DC albums bear the Vanda & Young stamp. Vanda & Young also produced brother John Paul Young's chart topper, *Love Is In The Air,* and have since returned to recording again, for Ensign, as pop group Flash & The Pan.

The long years between 1963 and 1974, when Angus was finally able to leave school, almost coincided with two of Rock music's most innovative periods, and what percolated through to them from the world outside Australia complemented the congenial home atmosphere and gave direction to their energy. It enabled them to set their musical sights, and life in a confined cage, when they were white hot, electric, ready to Rock, became unbearable.

The sounds that beckoned to them had to be filtered through the Australian media, a far from satisfactory process. Even in the late 60s Australia was a completely 'straight', culturally unimaginative and simplistic country. The best it had been able to offer—Frank Ifield, Rolf Harris, the Seekers—catered for an older family audience, and Australian television and radio preferred to promote this 'safe', 'wholesome' sound.

Two of Europe's leading Rock culture figures of the 'Psychedelic Era' were Australians who had been excommunicated by the Oz authorities for their ideas and their writings. Though both have today disappointingly moderated their views and appear to be working within the 'establishment view', Richard Neville, with his powerfully subversive London-based magazine, *Oz,* and Germaine Greer, during her 'Underground' days the editor of the sexually-liberating Amsterdam-based magazine, *Suck,* had as much genuine impact as the best Rock'n'Roll band of their day. But, six or seven years ahead of AC/DC, they had to leave Australia to achieve this.

Australia was then at least 10 years behind Britain, and 20 years behind the States, in terms of social emancipation. The 'battles' that had had to be waged in the US and then in Europe, yet had to be fought. But in this respect the Young brothers arrived on the scene in time to *benefit,* because they were undoubtedly in the front line of battle and could capitalize on the conflict; they were able to jump straight into the public eye and directly capture the admiration of kids like themselves. If they had stayed in Scotland, the story

would not have been so glamorous.

A glittering tour in the late 50s of Rock heavyweights Little Richard, Eddie Cochran, Gene Vincent, Buddy Holly and Australia's own Johnny O'Keefe and others, left the continent with scarcely any impact having been made. This was the tour on which Little Richard, standing on Sydney Harbour Bridge, announced his retirement from Rock'n'Roll to the world. He said he was going to devote his life to God. Of course, he didn't—not for long, at least—but he went so far as to take his treasured rings off his fingers and fling them into the sea. He made Rock'n'Roll history, and he made it in Australia.

Johnny O'Keefe was probably the first *true* Oz Rock star. Like Cliff Richard and P.J. Proby in Britain, he started out in the early 60s as an Elvis imitator, playing numbers like *Shake, Baby, Shake/Real Wild Child.* But the pressure to conform must have been too great. Unlike his British counterparts he eventually 'matured', joined the club circuits, and died. After him, apart from Pop bands like the Easybeats, and clone bands that mimicked American values, the bigotry and apathy of the Australian media caused a big void, until 1974.

But Australians couldn't consider themselves exempt for long, and genuine s-e-x-u-a-l liberating Rock'n'Roll, like elsewhere, had to be accepted. Imported Rock kept its hold—Chuck Berry, Little Richard, B.B.King, Aretha Franklyn, The Who, especially Pete Townshend's guitar and Little Richard's voice,

had a powerful effect on Angus Young; Fats Domino, Ike & Tina Turner on Malcolm. A 50s number like *Night Time Is The Right Time,* by Ray Charles and Marjorie Hendrix, with its combination of Gospel fervor and Rock, probably also had an influence, if indirectly, through Led Zeppelin. The Heavy Metal sound epitomized in AC/DC takes the 'call and response' of colored gospel and welds it on to the characteristic harsh, urban, working man Boogie Rock sound.

The late 60s music of Cream, Deep Purple, Black Sabbath, Hendrix, the Yardbirds and Led Zeppelin, in turn had its effect. These bands were the precursors of Heavy Metal. By late 1973 Led Zeppelin were already world class, and were embarked on their biggest-ever 32-city tour of the States—the one on which they broke the Beatles' attendance record at Shea Stadium— and it must have seemed to Angus and Malcolm that if they didn't hurry and throw off their restraints, they would miss their chance. But as I have tried to suggest, for *AC/DC, in Australia,* the timing for their launch was about right. All they needed to take the world title for themselves was gargantuan amounts of self-punishment.

Malcolm Young, being the first out of school, initially set the pace. He was born 6 January, 1953, in Glasgow, and though normally considered one of the quiet members of AC/DC, is generally assumed to be the brains behind the band's unmistakable intense sound. Thus his nickname, 'Riffmaker'.

Angus and he had actually taken up guitars independently, and had formed their own bands in Sydney, with little success—Malcolm playing in a number of Sydney Boogie Rock bands. But by the end of 1973 both brothers realized the potential of combining forces, and had formed a 'band' of their own. This was a very nascent AC/DC. Now Malcolm had literally to wait days for his kid brother to be unleashed, to turn it into the kind of band they wanted.

Their first performance was on New Year's Eve, 1973, in a small Sydney club called Chequers. Angus played lead, Malcolm rhythm. They did Rocking, raucous riffs and high speed Boogie to a receptive, wildly enthusiastic audience intent on seeing 1974 through double-glazed vision. Angus Young: "We had been together about two weeks. We had to get up and blast away. From the moment 'Go' it went great. Everyone thought we were a pack of loonies... you know, 'Who's been feeding them kids bananas?'."

AC/DC were largely inspired by their determination to kick against the traces of their claustrophobically staid upbringing in Australia. They were considered an outrageous, bad-boy band, renowned for their deafening onstage antics and subsequent backstage 'obscenities'. In fact, the back cover of their first UK album, HIGH VOLTAGE, features spoof letters to the band, including a severe note from brothers Angus and Malcolm's headmaster complaining about their 'abusive language and obscene gestures', and a love letter from a former conquest to singer Bon Scott warning him her father was planning to erase his flamboyant tattoos by pulling both his arms off!

Their very choice of name was a source of controversy with its bisexual connotations (unfounded, as it happens), and led to a memorable conflict with the head of a famous publishing company when he followed superbutch Bon Scott into the toilet one day and had his unwelcome advances spurned by a torrent of piss from the angry Bon.

Unlike so many other chest-beating Heavy Metal macho merchants, AC/DC have not made the mistake of taking their image too seriously. Angus's predilection for dressing as a wayward schoolboy onstage may have started out as a joke on his tender years when the band first formed, but that infamous character in cap, blazer and short pants has given AC/DC not only a visual focal point for their fans but also ensured that the band retain their basically fun identity. After all, how can anyone onstage get too carried away with their own ego while little Angus is maniacally whirling around like a demented sixth-former with sweat and snot cascading from his perpetually flailing head? (Atlantic Press Release, August 1981)

From the start, AC/DC had an attitude of hammerdown. The plan of conquering the world would be by the direct, traditional route of constant touring, straight into the eyes and ears of those who wanted their sound. From the start they regarded themselves primarily as a club band. In the clubs they could engage their fans head on. There would be no condescending bullshit, no contrived spectacle, but honest, hard working fun. This was a policy which fitted their temperaments for sincerity.

> # We're still as raw as the day we started.

Angus: "Too many bands rely on special effects to see them through. Apart from a bit of dry ice we don't have anything you could term 'special effects'.

"Everytime I ever saw a band they seemed so untouchable they never seemed completely real. We've been determined to steer away from that. We're real. We're still as raw as the day we started. That gives people value for money. For so long now fans have been subjected to second rate bands. Kiss, who only filled a gap left by Bowie, Nugent and Van Halen who filled a gap left by Zeppelin. People want the real thing, not imitations. That's why bands like the Who can still sell out Madison Square Garden for a week, whereas Kiss can't. Those bands simply used the time in between the tours of bigger groups to their own advantage. They weren't doing anything new. But AC/DC has a definite image, a definite style. We don't fill any gaps. Oh sure, if Zeppelin had toured every week we probably wouldn't have done so well. But we've always thought we were in the first division, even when we were playing small clubs back in Australia. We never wanted to compete with the local bands—we wanted to compete with the world."

They decided they would tour *blitzkrieg* fashion, concentrating their forces on one territory, conquering it after relentless, nightly assaults, then switching to a new target. Each new territory would be bigger, or more difficult to take, than the last. This was a policy which fitted their temperament for success.

By far their most difficult territory was the first. Quite apart from the simple fear shown by most older Australians to Rock Music, especially to the detrimental effect it might have on their hard-won lifestyles, there were other major factors—still peculiar to Australia today—which served to inhibit the growth to national or international status of any act. These were Australia's geographical isolation, and the structure of its mass media.

Most Australian Rock acts are condemned to achieve no more than local status not because of the absence of talent or lack of bands but because of the country's size, its lack of population and its remoteness from Western markets. The investment capital required to fund original touring acts within Australia, where vast distances hold disproportionately small populations, is considered by record companies to be prohibitive. New acts possessing integrity are automatically prejudiced, and only those with herculean determination to succeed will obtain appreciable inter-state followings. International stardom is reserved for psychophantic acts like the Little River Band (now thoroughly American, performing songs with American sentiments, e.g., *Going Home To Memphis*), family Pop acts... and the toughest of the tough.

Angus Young

Bon Scott

Malcolm Young

Mark Evans

Phil Rudd

This situation is the exact reverse of that found in Europe, the UK and the USA, where large, concentrated populations and long-established business patterns make it easier to find finance. Of course, finding finance is always difficult if you're poor and view things differently to the Status Quo.

The other obstacle, the structure of the country's mass media, is double-edged, working both for and against the artist. Australian radio shares at least equal power with the nation's television. It arbitrates public taste, and the hundreds of local and national radio stations vie with each other for lowest common denominator music. The small band with original material to offer is again the loser. But because of the Australian dependence on radio many local stations are truly community spirited, and do give air space to small bands—probably more, at a local level, than similar bands elsewhere receive.

God-given impediments and the Rock industry

Ian 'Molly' Meldrum, the director/host of Countdown, the country's television Pop and Rock program, is generally considered to be *the* arbiter on popular music. His program has a much more powerful effect on Rock consumption than its counterparts in the West, but once again there is little help given to original Oz acts who are poorly presented alongside flash, professionally produced imported film acts.

To an impartial observer the view from the bottom upward in Australia, New Years Eve, 1973... the climb AC/DC took through bigotry, incomprehension, fear, God-given impediments and the Rock industry, such as it was... would have looked impossible. But I don't believe that AC/DC looked. They set their sights on their target, without thinking too hard about the trajectory, and put the hammer down.

During the relentless bar and club gigs which followed the Chequers' party, the AC/DC line-up changed several times, eventually crystalizing out as Bon Scott (vocals), Phil Rudd (percussion), Mark Evans (bass), as well as Angus and Malcolm. With the exception of Cliff

Williams' replacement of Mark Evans on bass, in 1977, this was the line up AC/DC were to retain until February 1980.

Mark Whitmore Evans was an Australian who had attended the same school as Angus. Phil Rudd was "nearly born 19 May, 1954, in Melbourne, in the back of a delivery van..." and claims he has had a life-long score to settle ever since. He joined the band after gaining experience in several local bands in Melbourne, where he first came to AC/DC's attention.

By now, Angus and Malcolm had moved their base from Sydney to Melbourne, and the band were living together in one dilapidated house—a strong sign of the seriousness and shared sense of purpose which they had, and a habit they continued.

Melbourne was a sound choice in many ways. Next to Sydney it is Australia's largest city, and is probably *the* center of Rock'n'Roll in Australia. The band's track record laid down here, especially in traditionally 'strong' areas like Carlton, near Melbourne's University, which had been a spawning ground for generations of Oz bands, probably gave a dramatic impetus to its reputation.

The most significant occurrence during this period was of course the addition to the line up of Bon Scott. Hard-drinking, hard-living, gravel-throated Bon, hired as a roadie in Adelaide, during the Sydney days came to Melbourne because he sensed his chances in front of the mike. His verbal qualification was delivered to Angus, who readily agreed to hiring him.

"We knew Bon could sing better than he could drive, so the guy who managed us at the time asked Bon to join the band, and it really worked out very well. We used to have this singer who was a bit of a Gary Glitter freak, so he wouldn't have lasted long anyway. We had a bit of a blow with Bon and for the first gig the only rehearsal we had was just sitting around an hour before the gig, pulling out every Rock'n'Roll song we knew. When we finally got there Bon downed about two bottles of Bourbon with dope, coke, speed, and says, 'Right, I'm ready', and he was too. He was fighting fit. There was this immediate transformation and he was running around yelling at the audience. It was a magic moment. We were just about in the middle of a tour break, the first we'd had in ages, it seemed, so we partied for a week celebrating the new addition to the band."

"When I sang I always felt that there was a certain amount of urgency to what I was doing. There was no vocal training in my background, just a lot of good whiskey, and a long string of Blues bands, or maybe I should say 'booze' bands. I went through a period where I copied a lot of guys, and found when I was singing that I was starting to sound just like them. But when I met up with Angus and the rest of the band, they told me to sound like myself, and I really had a free hand doing what I always wanted to do.

"Those earlier cuts were nowhere near as raunchy as what I can do now (1977). The audience eats it up! You get on that stage, and the more crass, gross and rowdy you sound, the more they love it. So I just go up there and scream away, sometimes to a point where I can't talk the next day."

"I was earning a bit of spare money at the time working as a chauffer. One day, I was hired to drive AC/DC. I took the opportunity to explain to them how much better I was than the drango they had singing for them. So they gave me a chance to prove it, and there I was."
(Bon Scott, 1976)

Bon was AC/DC's most serious 'loony', rivalling Angus's stage performance with a zany, exuberant lifestyle that was often wreckless, sometimes dangerous. But he was just what AC/DC needed, both as singer to develop their Heavy Metal sound, and as a burly 'set-off' to Angus's mad schoolboy theatrics. I suppose you could say, in a fictive stage sense strictly, he became Angus-the-schoolboy's dad, or at least his protective elder brother, and completed the band's odd, appealing image.

His voice had power and command, engaging directly with the audience, but wasn't fully developed, as he humorously observed:

Like Angus and Malcolm, Bon was another emigré from Scotland. He was born Ronald Belford Scott, 9 July, 1946, emigrating to Australia with his family when he was five years old. Like Angus and Malcolm he quickly got frustrated with the Australian ways, and like them he found his answer in Rock'n'Roll and Rock culture, but his was a more chequered career—perhaps because of his age, coupled with his misfortune not to have been able to find AC/DC sooner. AC/DC's road crew referred to him affectionately as 'The Old Man', but despite his elder status in the band he was the one most careless for his own safety. The others often had to watch him to make sure he didn't get too excessive on account of booze, or into too many fights on account of his short temper.

Before he met AC/DC he had chauffered for other bands, and played as singer/drummer with various Rock bands, R'n'B and other groups of the late 50s and early 60s. These included a Country & Western outfit (he was the singer),

'bubblegum' Pop band the Young Valentines, and an Aussie Scottish pipe band. He was with the latter for five years, until the age of 16.

He had also painted ships, been in jail for two years on a charge of assault and battery, and been pronounced 'socially maladjusted' by the Australian Army. While Angus was still a toddler, Bon was beginning a kind of early 'drop out' lifestyle in the raw of the early 60s, influenced by hard street music from England and probably by the compelling, existential lifestyle of the American Beats of the 50s, which was then having its catalytic effect on British society and would soon mutate into the even more potent, colorful, extravagant 'Acid' Rock revolution of the later 60s—Hendrix, Cream and the rest.

In those halcyon days, but in Melbourne where his behaviour was less understood, dressed in psychedelic apparel and his body crawling with brilliantly-colored tattoos, Bon the showman walked the streets with a pet boa constrictor round his neck. He was one of the daring few who first helped shock conservative Australians into slow acceptance of youth independence, and when AC/DC came along it was the best opportunity he'd had to take his private rebellion to its limits. In return, he plugged a youthful Heavy Metal band into his own wealth of experience—not far off the bedrock of Rock'n'Roll.

The new combo brought tighter business management. The band gradually achieved recognition under the watchful eye both of its management, and Albert Productions—the George Young and Harry Vanda production team who had encouraged them from the start. The procedure George Young adopted was to 'vet' the raw compositions brought to him by Malcolm and Angus.

Angus: "He'd take our meanest song and try it out on keyboards with arrangements like 10cc or even Mantovani. If it was passed, the structure was proven, then we took it away and dirtied it up."

(like the explosive *She's Got Balls*)

As well as producing AC/DC's albums Albert Productions had geared themselves up to releasing them. They had formed a distribution deal with EMI's Australian subsidiary and the band's first two albums appeared under a joint EMI/Albert Productions Label. HIGH VOLTAGE was released first, in 1974, and contains a strong selection of the songs they were performing on tours, including the standard Blues number *Baby Please Don't Go.* On tour a fair percentage of their material was original, the rest being frenzied, wound-up arrangements of Blues, R&B and Boogie standards. On the original numbers (like the explosive *She's Got Balls*) which gradually predominated at performances, Angus and Malcolm usually wrote the music, and Bon the words, initiating a working pattern that remained fairly constant for many years.

Their second album, TNT, released in 1975, strengthened sales of the first album, and the results of almost two years of gruelling tours and deals were finally rewarded as both albums hit number one spots across Australia, winning Platinum, Silver and Gold discs for the band.

During these two years they had kept faithfully to their policy of playing to the audience instead of at it, and they had allied this with their ambition for success. The result was a far more spectacular and more sudden success than they had anticipated, and to continue logically with their plans, at the end of 1975 they were forced to look to the larger markets.

CHAPTER TWO

"I used to wear shorts because they were easier to get around in, instead of jeans. When you'd sweat a lot, they'd cling and stick to your legs. So I figured I'd take a hint off footballers and wear a pair of shorts. From that me sister came up with the idea, 'Why don't you just put your school suit on?' You see, I was going to school in Sydney at the time, and I had me school blazer, 'cause kids there wear uniforms. So I got an old cap, put a big 'A' on it, and there it was!

"When I first put on the schoolboy suit I thought, 'Well, you must look crazy in this school suit and everything, so you've got to show something else. You can't just walk on and expect everything to happen.' So I just kept adding to the act, and it got more and more outrageous. But I always had that walk and hopping thing. I just can't play if I've got to stand still. And ever since I can remember, I've always moved me 'ead when I heard music."

> ## I just can't play if I've got to stand still

The school uniform became a must for Angus, but in the beginning he also tried a gorilla suit, a Zorro outfit, and even a 'Super-Ang' get-up. As is usually the case the 'best' turned out to be the most obvious, and the most natural. But before we go further with AC/DC's story, a word about this demented schoolboy persona (AC/DC intellectuals and future puzzled historians of Rock'n'Roll take note).

We have so far taken Angus Young's stage image, and what it could possibly mean to the world's myriad AC/DC fans, for granted, without analysis. The mad schoolboy will be recognizable to English fans, and in countries where English culture has been imported. But to others, and maybe even to some contemporary British kids, it will not have a specific meaning. Nor will it matter to most: it's the music we want, not a theatrical treatise. But the fact remains that this unlikely and surreal image has played a significant part in AC/DC's rise to superstardom—it's the peg they hung

their music on—and it had a peculiar and timely effect on world youth.

First, the Angus Young (how appropriate that last name; prophetic) schoolboy look *is* distinctly English: the scruffy little tike, the bane of a thousand mothers, the fascinating tormentor of a million little girls. His socks are constantly bunched around his ankle, his school cap is always positioned *wrong,* atilt, worn on the side. You know that his nose is always full of snot and that he wipes it off on his dirty, mucus-covered sleeve cuffs. He carries pieces of string and live frogs in his pockets. And he never goes anywhere without a matchbox acrawl with caterpillars. He likes to piss on passing dogs and in mail boxes. In short, he's a little bugger.

The fascinating tormentor of a million little girls

So where did this Angus Young schoolboy come from? The obvious answer is that he came from experience. From the childhood of the Brothers Young. When the British came over to settle they brought with them their shared culture, among it books like *Tom Brown's Schooldays.* The school prototype is Kipling's *Stalky & Co* (1899), but the most popular of all these books was Frank Richard's 'Greyfriars' books, with their hero Billy Bunter. Richard's bastardized version of Kipling's book exerted tremendous influence, but as well as being a 'cozy' view of school life, it was also a very English middle-class one. The heroes of these stories were largely the sons of monied families, with the 'bullies' and the 'cads' coming from the lower classes.

It was the 'lower class' kids that formed the Angus-Young-schoolboy forerunners in the 1920s, in Richmal Crompton's 'Just William' books. This series was immediately and extremely popular, and ran into many books. One look at Just William and there is that 'bad boy' image of Angus Young—minus the guitar and the 'ead bangin'. But the world has moved on some from Crompton's day, and William's bad behavior now strikes us as laughable, even lame. These days he'd be down as the class faggot in terms of outrage. But nevertheless, though no English schoolboy has dressed like him for over 20 years, William remains forever the delinquent schoolboy, and the one that Angus Young has directly capitalized on.

The wayward schoolboy is, too, very much a part of traditional English music hall. Schoolboy characters have been present in English music hall for at least 50 years, the most famous being Jimmy Clitheroe, a dwarf from Oswaldtwistle, England, who still portrayed an adolescent schoolboy up until his death at the wizened age of 66. At the time of writing, a duo called the Krankies are one of the top acts in English clubland. In this act, the character—Wee Jimmy—is played by a diminutive woman in schoolboy drag... I wonder what Angus would say to this?

But the last believable manifestation of the world of 'Just William' (cast in a tougher and more modern setting) in the UK was in the 50s,

in English children's comic, *The Beano.* With its companion comic, *The Dandy,* this paper is still an English institution, with weekly sales of the two comics running into the millions, and in the early 50s, before television took over, British kids everywhere devoured it.

There are two links with Angus Young's creation here. The first lies in the English comic strip *Dennis the Menace* (not a bit like the more whimpish, middle-class American 'bad boy' Charlie Brown), about an anarchic schoolboy. Dennis came into his own in the early 50s. Then, in 1954 he was joined in *The Beano* by a whole classful of gleeful anarchist school kids, in the strip *The Bash Street Kids.* This strip of comic mayhem was created, scripted and drawn by one Leo Baxendale, himself then a young man in his early 20s. Baxendale was more in touch with the rebellious nature of kids

in the 50s than his peers, and within the restrictive policies of English comics his kids ran wild, took the piss out of teacher, even played Rock'n'Roll, and he must be credited with creating the first Rock'n'Roll strip schoolboy—*Teddy*—named after English Rock fans known at the time as Teddy Boys.

But the Bash Street Kids were the last of their kind, and by the late 50s *nobody* dressed like Young's 'bad boy'. The type was killed off forever by the more delinquent version of the bad kid from America—the kids from the *Blackboard Jungle,* Elvis and James Dean types. Suddenly children woke up to the fact that they were being dressed in ridiculous costumes by their parents, and after 1955—the advent of Rock'n'Roll in England—kids all over the world began to question the view of the world presented to them. Largely, they took the

Little Orphan Annie with an electric dildo

stance that their parents didn't know chicken-shit from rice about how to dress. Boys knew girls wouldn't fuck them if they dressed in short pants, so almost overnight England lost her little boys. No self-respecting kid, even a six year old, would be seen out on the street dressed like Angus Young.

Angus Young, of course, knows this. *His* demented schoolboy version is *macabre*— simply because he has taken such an innocent school character and made it work in the sex, drug, violence excess of 1970/80's Heavy Metal. Like Rupert Bear with a big dick, or Little Orphan Annie with an electric dildo.

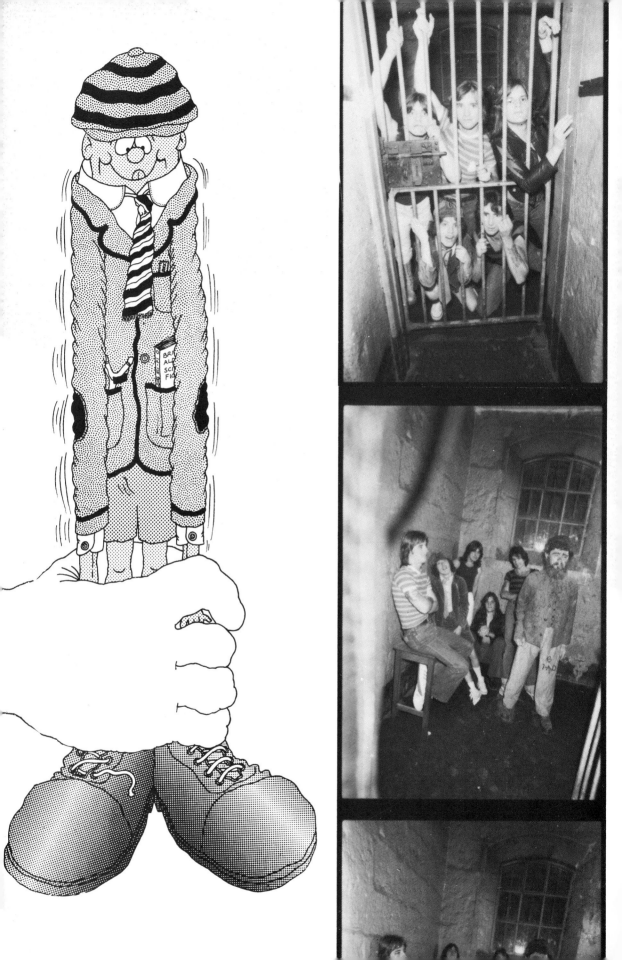

KODAK SAFETY

Then what is the appeal of the Rocked-out schoolboy? The fact that the 'Just William' character is no longer potent, and that AC/DC are liked in spite of this in places as unfraternal as Europe, Japan and the US (who knows, even the USSR?), where there can be little or no cultural understanding of the figure, leads me to believe that it is simply down to absurdity and paradox.

There is a compelling sexual fascination about the absurdity of corrupt innocence—the grown man dressed like a youth. AC/DC's music—powerful, sinister, adult—delivered through the hands of someone who seems to be a kid. But whatever it is—and the band constantly sabotage any serious attempts at analysis—there is no doubt that just now there is a strong yen among the world for the AC/DC mythos.

There is a compelling sexual fascination...

It must take a suspension of belief for American teenagers of the 1980s to realize that the streets of England were once full of kids dressed like Angus Young. In America, the 'tough kid' is best remembered from films featuring 'Our Gary', and later the 'Dead End Kids', from the Bogart film, *Angels With Dirty Faces.* The Dead End Kids metamorphosized into the Bowery Boys. But it would be incongruous to cast the 'bad boy' of Angus in their company—his origins are so obviously English. In any case, American kids have always been dressed as small adults. They did not have a two-nation-in-one that so divided British kids and which helped produce such a marked 'generation gap' as is found there.

Mostly, I suspect, Americans don't even connect the stage persona with a past reality. They believe that Angus Young alone invented that surreal, demented, loony character they see onstage.

CHAPTER THREE

Early line-up (1973-1977). From left to right: Malcolm Young, Mark Evans, Phil Rudd, Angus Young, Bon Scott.

Tour and conquer tactics

The crowded, 'working class' urban areas of Britain like Glasgow, Manchester, Newcastle and Birmingham, had an established Heavy Metal audience that had grown out of the Cream/Yardbirds years and was still being sensitized and developed by heavyweight British bands like Deep Purple, Black Sabbath and world leaders Led Zeppelin.

White Australia's roots, as well as Malcolm's, Angus's and Bon's, were in Britain, and England was regarded as *the* birthplace of modern Rock'n'Roll. It was natural and expedient therefore for AC/DC to want to come to Britain first. British success means a great deal to Angus Young for yet another reason:

"To me that (BACK IN BLACK going straight to the top of the UK charts) means so much because I've always regarded Britain as a credible place, much more so than America or anywhere else. In America you can hype a band to be successful, you take TV ads and show them off, like Kiss, and so on, and you can hype people into believing they're good when in fact they're not. But in England the fans see through all that and you have genuinely *got* to be good. So hearing it was number one was a really big thing for us because it meant we had beaten all the New Wave and the Rolling Stones... all of 'em.''

As in Melbourne, on their arrival in London the band moved en masse into one house. They were a virtual unknown quantity, but once again that habit of remaining in such close, personal contact with each other undoubtedly enabled them to organize their by now characteristically strong and coherent musical assault. They would use the same 'tour and conquer' tactics as they had in Australia, and as they would soon do in America, allowing only the idiosyncrasies of the British industry to vary the format of approach.

One of the most oft-repeated facts about AC/DC is their celebrated first appearance in Hammersmith, West London, at the small public bar known as the Red Cow early in 1976. Their act, so legend goes (helped a bit by Atlantic's copywriter) resembled a fast-moving fire, and by the second set the place was "filled to overflowing as patrons lit up the London switchboard with calls to their friends". Really? I doubt whether the entire residents of Hammersmith could accomplish that! Nevertheless, AC/DC's appearance had an indisputedly electric effect. For the first time a British audience was exposed to the sheer force of this new, Aussie sound.

Moving about like an electrocuted mannikin

To the bar room patrons it was like listening to Led Zeppelin on 'speed'. They had heard nothing like it before. The impulse to laughter at the sight of a schoolboy moving about like an electrocuted mannikin, with his fingers shooting like white-hot uranium bars up and down his guitar strings, and his head jerking like an epileptic spasmo caught in a permanent trauma, was cut in the throat by the thunderous, note-perfect delivery and Bon's screaming vocals. Bon's humorous attempt to grapple with the bagpipes, no doubt intended to display the band's links with Britain, heightened the sense of the absurd. Then, at the appropriate moment Angus leaped on Bon Scott's shoulders and, still hammering away at his guitar, was transported through the surprised, jubilant crowd.

The 'walk-a-bout', as this last feature of their act came to be known, though new to the

London audience, was by now a well-rehearsed routine. It was an outward show of fun that made the band 'accessible' in a real sense to its fans, and in Britain as in Australia, it became an essential part of the show.

Before touring on a large scale AC/DC made other debut appearances, including a whole string of dates at the fabled Marquee Club in London's red-light district of Soho. For a time they became the club's resident band, reputedly setting new attendance records at each weekly session. The gigs eventually drew upwards of 1,000 people at a time, filling to capacity a room that officially was able to hold no more than 700.

One of the most important first requirements in England was the support of a large record company operating in the Heavy Metal Rock field, both to act as a sympathetic financial advancer for their tours, and to ensure effective co-ordination of record releases. Before they left Australia they had commenced negotiations with the record company to whom Led Zeppelin was then signed, Atlantic Records. Atlantic had seen the band's Australian achievements, and now, after the success of the initial British gigs, signed AC/DC to a world-wide contract.

Lock up your daughters

The first tour proper was billed, provocatively, as the 'Lock Up Your Daughters Tour'. AC/DC's song title, *She's Got The Jack,* is polite phraseology for the retort, 'She's got the clap', and it is fair to say that the directly sexual subject matter of some of AC/DC's songs, as well as the band's often bawdy stage behaviour and, at this time Bon Scott's off-stage reputation, combined to give a real 'risque' image to parents concerned about their daughters' virginities. AC/DC had rightly and deliberately cultivated a licentious image as part of their fun-rebellion—it had been mainly this that had got up the noses of Australian parents and schoolteachers—and later, in France, their debauched reputation travelled ahead of their venues, causing some local French papers worried about the 'pox' to print leaders warning young girls from going near the band.

After the UK tour the band made their first highly successful tour of Europe. They had been fortunate in obtaining a support deal with Ritchie Blackmore's Rainbow. Rainbow had only recently broken from the legendary Deep Purple, and with Blackmore's reputation as Deep Purple's 'Jimmy Page', drew capacity crowds providing AC/DC with tremendous initial exposure.

In December they returned to Australia for a triumphant 26-date tour, and remained there during the first two months of 1977 to record their album, LET THERE BE ROCK.

It was the culmination of a year in which the band had been almost as busy travelling and recording as they had travelling and live-Rocking. Their first UK album, issued in May from Atlantic, had been a compilation taken from the two Australian albums. Titled HIGH VOLTAGE, after their first album, all of Side One is taken from the TNT album. Side Two takes *TNT, Can I Sit Next To You Girl* and *High Voltage* from the same album, but includes *Little Lover* and *She's Got Balls* from the Australian version of HIGH VOLTAGE. The Atlantic edition has a different cover to the TNT album (which also included a lyric sheet).

A single, IT'S A LONG WAY TO THE TOP (IF YOU WANT TO ROCK'N'ROLL)/CAN I SIT NEXT TO YOU GIRL, taken from the album and released a month earlier in April, was perhaps a reminder to those who were listening that the band knew they still had a tough fight ahead of them, but weren't flinching.

The first previously unrecorded material to appear was on a single, JAILBREAK/FLING THING, released in July. Another release, in October, was HIGH VOLTAGE/LIVE WIRE, a belated single from the HIGH VOLTAGE album.

Rocker appeared on their next album, DIRTY DEEDS DONE DIRT CHEAP, released in December 1976. This album included mostly original material, or at least newly recorded material, and also another of their songs of wry declaration, *Ain't No Fun Waiting Round To Be A Millionaire.* A single, BIG BALLS/THE JACK, taken from the album, was released at the same time.

At the Sydney studios of Albert Productions for the recording of LET THERE BE ROCK (the band's fifth and best album to date) George Young encouraged Angus to new extremes of expression in order not to inhibit the band's music. From now on he was to be as manic and 'free' as he chose. If amps blew up in the middle of one of his songs, they were to keep playing. "There was no way," George later explained,

25

"we were going to stop a shit-hot performance for a technical reason like amps blowing up."

The response in England to the releases and tours had been good, and in December they interrupted their Australian tour to return to London to hold a packed one-night concert at the Hammersmith Odeon—the first of many such 'extra' Christmas dates they were to play for British fans over the coming years.

The warm rapport that AC/DC have always been able to develop with their fans is one of the prime 'ingredients' in the AC/DC 'formula'. They want to conquer, but they want to contribute as well; they wish to be liked and they wish to give value for money at their shows. It doesn't matter whether they're playing the Shea Stadium or a spit-and-dirt bar in a backwater.

Angus: "Most bands, even when they start out, still think of themselves as a big band no matter how many turn out to see them. We never used to consider ourselves as *supporting* this band or that band, we were *playing,* that's how we always thought of it. When we went on stage it was *our* stage and we didn't care whose name was at the top of the bill. We don't want to be Adolf Hitler or anything, but we do want to reach as many people as possible.

"We just get out there and Rock. If your amp blows up or your guitar packs it in, smash it up and pick another one. And that's how it always was with us. We can't even stop and tune up. Those kids are all wound up. A second or two seconds is too much for them. They've gotta have it.

"We could go on and just be dead bland and not try and involve the audience in anything, but you may as well just play like on the record and not bother to try anything new. We get most of our ideas from songs when we're playing live; so it's important from that point of view as well. You can tell, every now and then we'll just *blow,* and me, by accident, I'll learn something new. It's always by accident, it's just spontaneous. And so, that gets put back to the kids. When you're doing that kind of thing it keeps everything much fresher for everyone."

Malcolm: "We are a club band, even though we don't play clubs anymore, but I know a lot of big bands who would never survive playing a club gig. I think people watch us and say to themselves, 'Oh, look at those poor buggers, they think they're playing in a club', when we might be playing to 10,000 or 20,000 people. You can't help but sympathize with an act like that—it's as simple as that.

"Places like the Philadelphia Spectrum may seem too massive to really get an atmosphere in, but not so many years ago I was thinking that about the Glasgow Apollo or Hammersmith Odeon, London. Then, I wanted to get back to the Red Cow, or the Marquee, and just play with eight lights and two speaker columns!"

Brian Johnson (on joining the band in 1980): "The thing is, to the kids in the audience, AC/DC pose no threat. I mean, they can look up and say, 'that could be me. I could be that guitarist... and that singer, he doesn't look any smarter than me, in fact I look smarter than him. That rhythm guitarist, all he's got on is a pair of jeans, T-shirt and pumps', and that's what they're standing there for."

Malcolm: "As long as you stick to your original plan of what to do, which is simply just to play, then that's the whole bottom of it. Just to get up on stage and put on a good show, it doesn't matter what's being said or not said about you."

Bon: "We're on the crowd's side because we give 'em what they want, and everybody gets into our show—because it's a band/audience show; we're not like performing seals, we're all in it together."

Angus: "The only image we've ever had is what we really are. We never cover anything. I mean, if Bon's kissing a virgin down the room and someone spots him, well tough shit. Nobody can blackmail him.

"We can't just sit on our arses and say the world owes us a livin' because we've paid our dues. Me, I think if I fluff a note I'm robbin' the kids. You're gonna pour it all on until you drop. So even if they hate you they can still say, 'At least they tried'."

"Bounced around like a rabid kangaroo...

Good sales figures during and following the tours encouraged Atlantic to release a collector's 'maxi' single, with tracks taken from the DIRTY DEEDS album. Released in February 1977, and taking its title from the album, it contains *Dirty Deeds* and *Big Balls* as a double 'A' Side, and (on the reverse side) the ubiquitous *The Jack*.

Releases slowed down in 1977, while the band concentrated on touring. Earlier in the year dates were already being prepared for the band's first US tour, scheduled for the summer, and inbetween recording LET THERE BE ROCK in January and taking their first step on American soil, they had to consolidate their gains in between Europe and the UK.

DIRTY DEEDS DONE DIRT CHEAP was at the top of the European and UK charts when the band returned from Australia in March for their second tour of the UK.

The Sun newspaper's Rock columnist, Bob Hart, caught them at the Lyceum Theatre, London. Hart must have asked Bon about his role in the band, and Bon, with characteristic irony, told him that he was the band's poet. To the literal-minded journalist, though, Bon did not look like a poet. "Tattoos were curled extravagantly around both arms, and his fingers were, as usual, curled around a very full glass", and on stage "he was effectively outgunned" by Angus, who "bounced around like a rabid kangaroo, firing off Chuck Berry guitar licks."

The tour was immediately followed by a second European tour, this time with Black Sabbath—like AC/DC a big touring band, and always on the road in their early days (initially as the Earth Band). The tour was a huge success, forcing the realization that the next time AC/DC toured Europe they would headline.

At the end of June the band were unexpectedly concerned once more with line-up problems, caused by the abrupt departure of Mark Evans. Advertisements for a new bassist brought 50 responses, and from auditions of applicants, held in London, the band finally settled on experienced British player Cliff Williams, as their new choice.

Cliff was born 14 December, 1949, in Romford, England. He moved with his family to Liverpool when he was nine, where he spent the first two working years of his life as an engineer (at a factory in Upper Mill Street, behind Lime Street Station) before joining his first band.

By the time he was hired by AC/DC at the age of 28, he had achieved a substantial track record working with a number of English bands including Home and Bandit, and proved to be a reliable replacement of Mark Evans, remaining with the band to the present day.

After the auditions AC/DC returned briefly to Sydney to rehearse with the new line-up prior to their departure to the States.

They had taken less than 18 months to make their presence felt in Europe and Britain—six months less than they had taken to make the same impact in Australia.

CHAPTER FOUR

While the shores of America have only recently become a beach-head for AC/DC, the group has literally been tearing up the English/ European countryside with their no-holds-barred style of playing. They play a brand of Rock that can only be classified as Heavy Metal. With their amps turned way up, they thunder across the stage like a raging tornado about to engulf everything in its path. They are a whirlwind of sound, a time bomb ready to explode, given the slightest opportunity.

At the forefront of all this madness is the youthful Angus Young, whose steaming guitar work is positively awesome, an exercise in exalted mania. On stage, this compact performer (small in stature, but man-size in his ability to play) is in constant motion, bobbing his head up and down in jerking motions, while jumping about, making obscene gestures, stripping to the waist and finally going into what appears to be an epileptic fit, racing back and forth and scaling speakers as if he were King Kong climbing the Empire State Building.

At first you might be prone to laugh. But, once you've heard and seen him, you know better than to poke fun at him, as you realize it wouldn't take much for him to get excited and ram that guitar of his right up your ass.
Irving Sealey, "Hard Rock", 1978

There was no other market as big as the US one, and so success there was vitally important, particularly from the financial point of view. America would provide the band with the solid base to which the rest of the world Rock market could be subjugated.

The HIGH VOLTAGE and DIRTY DEEDS DONE DIRT CHEAP albums were already available to American audiences when AC/DC arrived, and had made a modest impact in the charts. But there was a definite need among the teenage young in the cities for a high energy live act. Led Zeppelin attracted mainly the 25-35 year age group, while Aerosmith (the other big US HM touring band of the late 70s) had a following composed mainly of late teen and 20-year-olds. AC/DC gathered an audience cross-section, but it was primarily the young and the very young who were attracted to the high-powered assured 'booze' music and the over-the-top head-banging.

The band therefore were greeted with a certain ready-made allure. To the uninitiated they were probably at first regarded as a Heavy Rock Punk hybrid, because their rise in the UK had been almost coincidental with the rise of the Punk movement. The general press—even the music press—had tended to lump them in the same bag. It is to AC/DC's credit that at a time when most of the British music press was preoccupied with the Punk and (later) the New Wave phenomenon, they continued to rate high in British reader polls.

Angus: "In those days we used to get called a Punk band. We used to do all these camp gigs where it was all pouftas, lesbians and yobbos called sharpies with dyed hair and big pants and big boots who'd come along to laugh at the pouftas."

Their act was probably outrageous enough to win converts off early Punks, or at least to win some shared attention, and this might have been one of the factors of their success, for Heavy Metal music was not fashionable in Britain at that time.

29

Whatever it was the American crowds liked, their delight at the first US gigs was generally in evidence. The tour started in the summer and ended in the winter. It was broken in the fall by a third tour of Europe as well as a third tour of the UK, and reached its peak at New York's Palladium and at the CBGBs club in New York's Bowery district.

Sylvie Simmons, writing for Sounds, reported that when the band performed before the cynical crowds at the Los Angeles Whisky gig, patrons were amazed by the act, which was among the most athletic they had seen.

After the first part of the US tour, while the band were touring Europe, AC/DC's fifth album, LET THERE BE ROCK, was released after lengthy delays. As usual there had been little time for recording. Nevertheless this was their most confident effort to date, packing some hard hitting songs like *Overdose, Bad Boy Boogie, Hell Ain't A Bad Place To Be* and *Go Down.* It immediately topped the European and UK charts. It also became the pivot of what success they managed to achieve in America, for when the band returned there in the late fall to start the second 'prong' of their tour, they found that the album had partly breached the magical FM airplay 'barrier' and had climbed encouragingly in the charts.

As expected, this time they toured Europe as headliners. On the accompanying UK tour the tenor of the times was again apparent in the choice of support act. At Sheffield they were supported by the Suburban Studs, a Punk band dressed in leopard-skin trousers, studded jackets and parachute jackets... which must have served to help detract from the image of themselves they wished to project.

But their stage material—*High Voltage, Whole Lotta Rosie, Problem Child* and numbers like *Crabsody In Blue,* their song about gonorrhoea—as well as the powered style of their performance, should have dispelled any doubts that they were Punks.

The constant touring meant they were continually learning to shape their act, honing it down. Angus had already started using a cordless, radio-controlled Kenny Shaeffer guitar, which simplified both his stage performance and his walk-a-bout routine. The cordless guitar was also safer to use.

"When I used to play with the cords they were always getting wound around the mike stands, and seeing them being retrieved after I'd been out in a crowd was like watching a life-saving team at work. Now I don't have those problems, and the cordless guitar is good, too, because you can get power and shock. At one of the US gigs

the whole stage was alive—and I was covered in water, getting belted from one side to the other. I threw the guitar, which my roadie caught, and he got thrown back against the wall. Eventually we had to switch all the power off. Imagine what it would have been like in Europe, where the power is 240 (in America it's only 110)?''

"Sexists led by a snot-nosed brat"

Not everyone liked the band, of course, or the way it was 'stirring up' the masses. Journalist Andy Gill, writing about the Sheffield gig in the NME, saw them as "4/4 monotony sexists led by a snot-nosed brat".

Much of the British music press was still trying its hardest either to slag off the band, or to ignore it, and as the band seemingly regardlessly carried on increasing its followers, many of the reviews became progressively more disdainful and dismissive, the silences more ridiculous (how was it possible to encounter a Rock'n'Roll holocaust-in-the-making and not *see* it?).

This disdain by influential sections of the press for Heavy Metal and 'Good Time' music, particularly personal attacks on the players, has been a sore point with AC/DC since their early days, and high feelings sometimes obscure from them what good press they *do* receive.

Brian Johnson (on joining AC/DC): "You know, the first thing Angus and Malcolm said to me when I joined this band? They said, 'Do you mind if your feelings ever get hurt?', and I said 'Why?', and they said, ''cause if you're going to join this band you're going to be expected to take fucking stick. Because we've always been slagged off by every fucking reporter since we left Australia'. And I said, 'Well, I'm going to have to take stick anyway, taking Bon's place'. But luckily these guys are so much like a family that you never get the chance to feel alone; like, you could just sit by yourself in your hotel room and feel like shit. They even start knocking dead people, and that really pisses me off. They thought they were being clever, but they don't realize that they're talking *about people,* and those people—the relatives and friends of Bon—have feelings. The lads say to me, 'Just fucking ignore them'. And that's what we do. We're *good* in our field. We just go out and don't give a fuck about critics. We play what we play and that's that''.

Bon Scott (October 1978): "The music press is totally out of touch with what the kids actually want to listen to. We've done six tours of this country and we *know*. These kids might be working in a shitty factory all week, or they might be on the dole—come the weekend they just want to go out and have a good time, get drunk and go wild. We give them the opportunity to do that."

Angus: "A lot of people tend to think of me as a one-style guitarist, but I can do different things—it's all really a matter of what you're trying to do or how you feel at the time. You know, Bo Diddley's been playing just two chords for something like 25 years or more. But it's the way he plays those two chords that counts. It's whether the thing is Rocking and Swinging that matters. It could be any amount of chords...

No gimmicks
No synthesizers

"We've got the basic thing the kids want— they want to Rock, and that's it. They want to be part of this band as a mass. When you hit a guitar chord a lot of the kids in the audience are hitting it with you. They're so much into the band, they're going through all the motions with you. If you can get a mass to react as a whole, then that's the ideal thing. That's what a lot of bands lack, and why the critics are wrong."

Their policy of ignoring the chauvinistic attitudes of the press was the only one they could take without sacrificing their aims of becoming a world class band who wished to remain true to their fans.

They began another year of touring and recording, with scarcely a break, and early 1978 found them back in Sydney at work on their new album—POWERAGE. The album was recorded fast—half the songs in one take—and was released in April.

Donna McAllister reviewed the album for Sounds, emphasizing the power and professionalism of the music. She is in accord with Angus Young's sentiments, but not perhaps in a way he would agree:

As song writers, Young, Young and Scott are hardly a Jagger/Richard, Lennon/McCartney or Plant/Page, and there are no Rock classics on this album. But this is skilfully disguised by the full-bodied group ravaging. The same basic thing applies lyrically; there is nothing profound or terribly quotable, but this has no real bearing on what this group most definitely is. Impact.

And by God, that is nothing to knock. Their impact has nothing to do with shock value, no sensationalist, yellow-journalistic, fashionable vagrance. No alienating gimmicks. *No synthesizers.*

These Australians have come through fighting—and winning—all the way. Listening to POWERAGE is barelling through track after track of non-retreatable battle. It is luring and nasty, from the opening track, *Gimme A Bullet,* the incessant thumping bass drum making the song (dare I say it?) danceable and clinging, all the way to the end of Side Two, *Kicked In The Teeth.* Each number unfolds into the next, keeping a flow constant as the tunes race by.

It's odd to note that the charges of sexism often laid against AC/DC's members have come from the pens of male critics. Female reviewers whose work I have seen appear to like the band for its honesty and lack of pretension, and they have laid no charges. Sexism implies deliberation on the part of the aggressor sex, and there is no indication of any such policy to be found either in AC/DC's work or in their public interviews.

POWERAGE was *power*—asexual and hermaphroditic—and heralded the year Angus & Co got their real taste of the world. With New York management Michael A. Browning, they now planned a massive itinerary of tours to build on the achievements of 1977.

The Powerage World Tour was 'born' 26 April with 28 major venues in the UK, including a show-case appearance at the London Odeon on 7 May. It continued growing through June (after a last UK date at Dundee's Caird Hall on 29 May) to October, with a marathon 76 date US tour. A dozen European gigs followed this, before a final tour of the UK in the fall.

It was the slickest, most prestigious and most spectacular tour the band had mounted. Merchandising included an AC/DC T-shirt emblazoned with a 3-color motif of a guitar, its neck apparently stabbing (or emerging from) a map of Australia, together with the band's logo

Angus's lead playing becomes cleaner and more authoritative. The whole band turns the screw relentlessly towards an optimum tightness which hopefully they will never reach because it will prove entirely too much for the human cranium. And the sound remains that bit different to all the rest because of the way the usual roles are juggled around: Cliff Williams plays bass like a rhythm guitar, strumming a constant deep thrum, while Malcolm Young on guitar plays the lead line straight and Angus either reinforces it or improvises around it.

The band, he thought, had improved. This time round the P.A. was up to scratch, enabling Bon's vocals to be heard properly for the first time. And Angus had a new set of front teeth to replace "the jagged disarray like tree stumps in a battlefield which used to be on view as he shook his head".

The venue, the Mayfair, with a capacity of 2,000, was sold out, and by the time the band returned there in November the ranks of fans had swollen, and AC/DC appeared on two consecutive nights.

and the tour legend, printed on pale blue. Yellow sweat shirts and clear perspex badges bearing the same design were also available, as were button badges, sew-on patches and stickers bearing only the logo, as well as a full color AC/DC poster.

The design of the tour brochure prefigured the cover and publicity for the band's long awaited live album, IF YOU WANT BLOOD YOU'VE GOT IT, recorded during the summer and released at the end of the US tour in October. There is blood everywhere, redness on almost every page. The brochure's jacket is clad in mock stage shots of Angus. On the front his body is shown punctured by a vengeful guitar neck, blood pumping from his stomach and mouth and all over his white school shirt. On the back cover he is depicted lying face down, slain, only now the stem has gone clean through his torso and projects from his blood-spattered back. In the battleground stands an eerie drum kit, silent and empty... There have been no witnesses to an appalling slaying by the instruments of Rock'n'Roll of a poor, innocent schoolkid who didn't know any better!

Phil Sutcliffe, the band's most serious and thoughtful reviewer, who has a real capacity to put their music and their act into perspective, caught the band twice during the year, both times at Newcastle, once at the beginning and once at the end of the Powerage tours. In May's Sounds he wrote:

The November act was dominated by "six black walls of amps and speakers, two pointing in at the band, four pointing out at the audience". Cliff Williams on bass, and Phil Rudd on drums, "carved out the sound" around which Angus and Bon weaved, while Angus's guitar was "clearer, less flashy than in earlier days". Angus had achieved a better "sense of his own style".

The set had opened with a "colossal guitar riff that battered the air" *(Live Wire)*, then went into *Problem Child, Sin City* and other numbers. "Here's an old family favorite," announced Bon, with a leer, part way, and the band began the "stripper's bump and grind of *She's Got The Jack,* gross, funny and bizarre". *Gone Shootin', Whole Lotta Rosie,* and the finale with Malcolm and Cliff "beating out the Chuck-Berry-for-a-nuclear-age riff of *Rocker",* followed, while Bon took Angus on a "gallop through the crowd". *Rock And Roll Damnation* and *Let There Be Rock* rounded off the set.

In Detroit, during the summer, the band encountered some of the official incomprehension it is accustomed to receive. They had been warned by the promoter to protect the ears of the screaming, rabid crowd (perhaps because of a State byelaw or because he thought his own sons and daughters were amok in their midst). He must have kept a pretty careful monitor of their act, for after five numbers when the act had really started to catch fire and the decibel level rose above 98, he 'pulled the plug'. Crowd, band and road crew were incensed, but AC/DC waited patiently through the mayhem that followed, until they had been paid . Then, according to the story I have, an enraged Malcolm Young vented the anger of all concerned by leaping up and sticking a full frontal nut on the guy's face. Threats of arrest subsequently issued by the promoter's outfit were countered with threats of a $15,000 writ for damages to the band's equipment. A disgusted band left amidst a stalemate.

Sylvie Simmons (Sounds, August) was at the Los Angeles Starwood during the tour. She wrote, "There's something about this band that can get you moving quicker than milk of magnesia." Many could believe her. Inside the auditorium she found a scene of bodies, fumes and resonation that resembed "a Ken Russell vision of Rock'n'Roll hell". During the performance Bon screamed the lyrics of *Whole Lotta Rosie* with a voice that sounded like it had "been in every bar Down Under, so raw it hurts". *She's Got The Clap* and *High Voltage* were other numbers the reviewer thought stood out. And bassist Cliff Williams helped add a fuller sound with his occasional backing vocals. Simmons finished: "Why can't more Rock'n'Roll bands be like this?"

In November, back in the UK, the New Musical Express, in an indulgent mood, allowed John Hamblett to cover the Sheffield gig. Hamblett gave the view from the 'Other Side'...

Hungry for a two hour slice of the sex and drugs and Rock'n'Roll dream cake

The gig. Yeah... we're in Sheffield, and I can't recall ever having seen so many bodies packed so tightly into such a comparatively small area; the crazy ones and the deliriously drunken ones jumping up and down, and shaking themselves like mad wet dogs, holding up the frailer ones.

Later, when things get really hog wild, this built-in safety mechanism falls short of requirements and bodies are frequently hauled out over the stage apron into the safety of the backstage area.

The crowd cheer anything and everything, setting up a big football type chant of 'ANGUS! ANGUS!', riding on each other's shoulders, waving their shirts in wild salty arcs over their heads, already sweating and steamy.

They're kids mostly, a neat cross-section of counter cultures: long-haired bairns with flarey jeans and distant vagueness in their eyes, and the washed-out tail feathers of the Punk scene with boutique-type leather jackets and school shirts and school ties.

All young, post-Hippy, post-acid, post-love and peace, Big Beat Niks, all hungry for a two-hour slice of the sex and drugs and Rock'n'Roll dream cake.

Not one of them looks like he or she gives a solitary damn about any pie-in-the-sky abstract questions of social relevance or contemporariness.

Hell, why should they? They've got real problems crowding up their heads, like what to do with Saturday night to make the rest of the week bearable?

Eno, Kraftwerk, Devo? Dogs, man, high fallutin' dogs. I mean, where's the fun in that? Where for Christ's sake is the spiky rolling-tank-track-straight-thru-brick-walls howling-at-the-moon BIGBEAT in that?

AC/DC, the outrageous Aussies, get into the only type of music that could conceivably gell with this outside, desperate, goodtime atmosphere; blistering and warping electric waves of hard nose music, a mish-mash of the most unholy influences imaginable.

Where the music is coming from is obvious. Where it ends I have not the foggiest notion.

It emanates, quite obviously, from the five young men on the stage—huge, heavy slabs of metallic sound that should hang in the air like steel webbed clouds, but don't. I feel the music must be absorbed by the bodies in front of me, but no visible signs of transformation are apparent...

...which is the elitist view again, and in some senses could be regarded as the Rock establishment view of AC/DC. But now it is the I-don't-like-it-but-it's-there-by-mass-consent-so-I-might-as-well-enjoy-the-spectacle view. When you are a low-level animal Nazi scum band and start getting reviews like that I guess you chortle to yourself and scratch your balls and know it is another sign that you have arrived.

But that is the UK. America is not the UK, and in spite of the good reception the band received on their first two tours they really only managed to set the fuse alight. It would take more than a couple of Herculean run-ups to ignite the explosions.

CHAPTER FIVE

"In the past we really never had much time to spend recording, because we were always on the road. So our albums tended to be very rushed. In fact last year we spent 10 months touring, and prior to that we hadn't had a break since the band began. We'd just go in and do the albums—which, of course, were mainly written on the road—and we never really had time to sit back and plan things.

"We took far more time over HIGHWAY TO HELL. We also used a different producer, which definitely helped. It was an experience for Lange, because he'd never worked on anyone as hard as us. We benefited more than anything from his work with Bon. We've always had our own basic style which hasn't changed that much, and in fact HIGHWAY TO HELL was all written and ready to record before Mutt came in."
Angus Young, 1979

As well as POWERAGE and IF YOU WANT BLOOD YOU'VE GOT IT (which was received extremely well everywhere, including the States) in 1978 Atlantic released two singles,

Hell ain't a bad place to be

ROCK'N'ROLL DAMNATION and WHOLE LOTTA ROSIE. The former, released in June midway between the two albums as a 'bridge', takes its title track from the live album, and *Sin City* (its reverse side) from POWERAGE. The single, WHOLE LOTTA ROSIE, appeared in November one month after the live album from which it takes both its tracks (r/s *Hell Ain't A Bad Place To Be*). But the next release of new

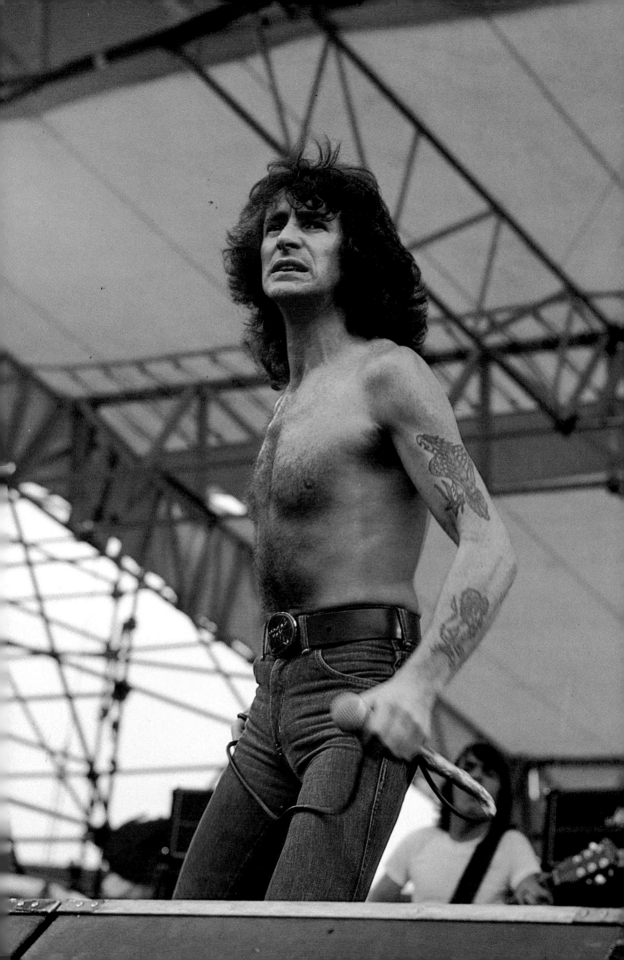

material was not until July 1979, a full year and a quarter after the release of POWERAGE, and the longest that fans had had to wait for a new album. The cause of the delay was not the band's usual one of lack of recording time (brought about by touring requirements) but resulted from a growing awareness among its members of the need to modify their raw sound with a more polished, melodic professionalism.

The difficulty of gaining strong acceptance in the States was perhaps the main stimulus behind this thinking, and the first positive move was made by Atlantic.

Bon: ''Initially, Atlantic wanted us to use another producer for a change. So they gave us a guy whose name I won't mention for political reasons. Anyway, it didn't work out, so in the end we got hold of Mutt Lange, who did City Boy and the Boomtown Rats. Luckily it turned out really well with him.''

Robert John ('Mutt') Lange also produced the Outlaws, Graham Parker and Thin Lizzy, and was chosen after unsatisfactory trials with several UK and American producers. Hiring Lange, of course, meant moving away from Vanda & Young, who had been the band's production cradle for so long. But Harry and George themselves genuinely felt that AC/DC needed to make a fresh move, and let them go. According to Bon there was no question of a permanent break with Albert Productions, for the band still regarded the Sydney team as an important part of their music, to whom they would return for certain projects and when the moment was right.

The move hadn't been made purely for ambitious reasons. The band had a constant need for new vigor and freshness, and when they felt, as they did, that they were stuck in a rut, they decided it would be better for everyone's sake to try something new.

Lange's studios were conveniently situated, at London's famous venue for Rock and Roll theater, the Roundhouse. This was just as well, for the hassles attendant on the changeover, as well as the commitment to improve musically, meant that the new album took six months to record—the longest time the band had spent on any album.

The album, HIGHWAY TO HELL, was released by Atlantic on 27 July, 1979, and it was evident immediately that the extra time spent on

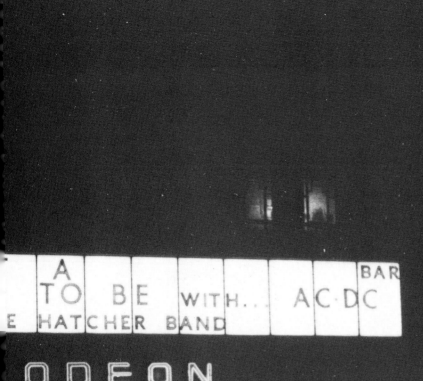

49

production had resulted in a record that was more sophisticated than previous attempts and that would receive a stronger reaction in the States, where radio audience tastes lean more to the Journey/Foreigner type M.O.R. sound than to the stripped down sound AC/DC were accustomed to.

Journalist Steve Gett, interviewing Bon Scott, thought that the band had managed to capture a sound "free from the somewhat empty feeling that dominated previous studio recordings". He thought Bon inevitably had to alter his studio technique, and Bon, who claimed that Lange had got him to project his voice more effectively, agreed.

"The bottom line is still very much hard Rock, but we've used more melody and backing vocals to enhance the sound. It's possible there is a more commercial structure to the music, without going the whole way. In the past, it's just been a total scream, so I worked on it a lot more this time."

On the fence between critics and fans

The album was reviewed with clarity by Dave Lewis, in Sounds (July 1979). Lewis is another regular writer on the AC/DC scene, but unlike Phil Sutcliffe seems to have started out disliking the band, and his reviews and articles contain an odd mixture of sentiments. He tires of the 'ridiculous' simplistic 'Chunga-Chunga' music which is still in evidence on HIGHWAY TO HELL, as well as the album's lyrics, which are in typical 'mysogynist' vein, but he is full of praise for the band for keeping up the HM genre 'sound' album after album while still managing to make it sound raw and exciting (unlike Kiss, who had succumbed to the Disco beat). He praises Angus in particular for, as usual, successfully holding the music together. His one serious complaint is that Bon still doesn't manage to do more with his voice other than bellow and roar (except on one track, *Love Hungry Man,* a song which features some vocal double tracking and which proved to Lewis that Bon could do something relatively fine with his voice).

He thought the band suffered the fate of all such highly stylized outfits, on the fence between critics and fans, wondering whether they dare risk alienating their fans by changing to something more credibly musical, or carry on pleasing the fans and risk the inevitable backlash from critics. Only a few such groups had managed to do both well—the Beatles and the Rolling Stones, for instance, whose music had always remained within the bounds of popular acceptability and yet had been daring and innovative. But equally few bands managed to play good genre music and keep up the pace year in and year out, and AC/DC were ranked among these few. Fifteen months later, at the band's Long Beach gig, California, when Lewis brought up the subject during interview, Angus emphasized AC/DC's intention to stay within the genre and their reasons for doing so.

"It's harder for a band like us because there's a lot of stuff we come up with that we have to reject. I mean, with a band like the Beatles, anything they thought of they could use because they went from one style to another. But with us, we're in this Hard Rock style, so what we try to do is look for things that are a little bit different without straying too far from our basic sound, 'cause there's nothing worse than trying to go above people's heads. I don't believe people grow with the music. When they first come to see you, that's when they identify with you, and if they like it, then that's what they want to hear more of."

To make sure that their intentions with regard to HIGHWAY TO HELL weren't misunderstood by the press, the band made themselves freely available for interview. Phil Sutcliffe caught them at the Swiss Cottage Holiday Inn, London, when they had given eight interviews (including Phil's) in 24 hours. He found them essentially unchanged.

Cosmopolitan life has done nothing to prettify the elongated Antipodean vowels which, if you catch the band all talking at once, make them sound like a herd of sheep or possible quintuplet Bugs Bunnies (Cliff Williams' cockney doesn't materially alter the tone). And Angus still has that slight catch and splutter in his voice which, when he was 16, I took to be caused by his tooth-brace, but is cackling away even now that he's put away such childish things.

The way he smokes a cigarette is probably more eloquent than anything he might say in proving he's come through the story so far with soul unscathed. You know how people *perform* smoking in various styles as if it were an art, craft, hard labor, a delicate surgical operation or even an athletic sport. Well Angus smokes as if he were awkwardly taking an illicit puff in the bogs at morning break.

The band's aims remained constant, and their sound had started markedly to change, away from its Rock 'Boogie' influence toward a more traditional Heavy Metal Sound, without becoming bland Middle-of-the-Road—a clever combination of Rock'n'Roll feeling and hard-nosed production sense that ensured their survival in the wider world market.

CHAPTER SIX

The remainder of 1979 was taken up with the Highway to Hell tours, in America and in Britain, but before these AC/DC had a date which Angus Young at least regarded to be of high importance.

Angus has long been an admirer of the Who's music as well as their atypical stage performance during their peak years, and he had therefore regarded it as an honour when AC/DC had been invited to support his former heroes at their Wembley Stadium open air gig that August. It is rare for Angus openly to admit to any guitar influence except Chuck Berry and Peter Townshend.

"I've not been influenced much by other guitarists. So far as listening goes I've always got off more on other instruments than the guitar. Things like saxophones and clarinets—they wail better. They don't just put their left foot forward, they get to the heart of the matter and sink their teeth in. I don't really listen to a lot of other music, but in terms of Rock, I like Townshend—I saw him at Nuremberg, and every time he swung his arms, he *did* hit his guitar! And I like Chuck Berry. Berry to me might play good on 364 days during the year, but on the 365th he can be great.''

The gig took place on the 18 th , with co-supports Nils Lofgren and the Stranglers. As was to be expected, squads of mods and older generation fans turned up. They probably saw the support bands as bonuses, but when it was AC/DC's turn to play they seemed genuinely impressed— if not by the Heavy Metal sound, at least by the tight professionalism. They gave the crowd one of their best performances, which was unfortunately marred mid-way by an embarrassing mishap.

They may never exactly be fashionable but AC/DC are in serious danger of becoming one of the world's great Rock bands. For illustration I'll just describe the fourth song in their set, a wonderful rendering of *Bad Boy Boogie*.

As if he thought matters had become a little tame to date (they hadn't) Angus *opened* the number by sprinting across stage, flinging himself on the floor and flailing himself round in circles all the while playing a berserk solo. OK, we were listening. Then AC/DC played the most inspiring hard and heavy you could imagine, so strong, so satisfying I'd even call it moving—the shivers and prickling of the scalp it gave me.

very silly they carried on screaming and stomping to themselves and must have been amazed to see the previously joyful crowd slow hand-clapping.

Anyway, when normal service was resumed Angus and Bon went walkabout on the terraces with the radio guitar and they encored by demand with *If You Want Blood,* which said it all for this earthy, honest, superb band.
(Phil Sutcliffe, Sounds, August 1979)

The change in production was followed by a change in management, from Michael Browning

The outstanding features were Bon's much developed vocals, the awesome tone of the Young guitars when in tandem (they reminded me of Southside Johnny's horns) and the intense authority of the rhythm section, Malcolm, Cliff Williams and Phil Rudd, who are clearly committed life, soul and sinew to every beat.

They sustained this high through *She's Got The Jack* and *Highway To Hell,* until half way through *Whole Lotta Rosie*—they were unmanned by a farcical technical hitch. To wit the entire PA was extinguished at a stroke and unbeknown to the band, still deluged in onstage sound from monitors and backline. Looking

to American mega-management company Leber and Krebbs, who also handled Blue Oyster Cult, Aerosmith, Ted Nugent and other Heavy Rock acts. Leber and Krebbs were able to sense AC/DC's potential as a world heavyweight, and from their more experienced and more influential position they were able to pull highly beneficial deals. The willingness of such a powerful management to sign AC/DC must surely have made the band feel that they were fast approaching super-star class.

Their hard work and initiative paid dividends on their return to America, where absence had served to heighten popularity. On their last tour they had been essentially a support band (for Journey), but on their new tour they were headlining for the first time. Support was by the likes of Sammy Hagar, Molly Hatchet and the Pat Travers Band, and AC/DC's no-holds barred music, because of its more commercial flavour, now got unreserved airplay by the nation's conservative radio stations.

Towards the end of their tour at the Long Beach, Los Angeles, gig, the band's act was reviewed again by Sylvie Simmons (Sounds, October 1979). Someone must have told her that 'Fun Rock' was supposed no longer to be in fashion, for like Dave Lewis she now berates the

collective dose of the clap and have a similar effect on the brain cells.

Like the man asked why he wanted to climb a particular mountain who answers 'because it's there', I'm drawn to this depraved quintet simply because they're here once again, and because amid this ever-changing universe they can be relied on to be much the same as last time.

The band continued to give lengthy interviews, even after gruelling performances when most acts of their status would refuse such generosity. Their minds were set on the future, and not on

Fast-approaching super-star class

band for its 4/4 'banality' while admiring its consistency. But, like Lewis, her enthusiasm is not dampened by her criticism:

As wonderfully seedy and solid a set as last year. Don't even ask me why I trudge to Long Beach again for the annual aural assault by a bunch of homeless Aussies who are about as subtle as a

the discomforts of the present. Two of their Texas gigs, Dallas and San Antonio, were covered by journalist Steve Gett (Melody Maker, November 1979) who was allowed by the band to travel with them in the tour bus.

Gett noted that Texas was one of the parts of America most heavily predisposed toward this onslaught of "Highland clan and Aussie aggressive determination", and as Angus observed to Gett, "When we come down to Texas it's a real journey into hell, not in the bad sense but basically because it becomes total mayhem! So I guess *Highway to Hell* is a pretty apt title for this leg of the tour".

The morning after the Dallas gig we set out on the lengthy journey to San Antonio on the band's bus, which—like most American tour buses—was well furnished with facilities to pass the time on the seemingly endless highways. The television, videos, a stereo and (more important) a number of bunks helped to diminish the ennui en route.

Conversation revolved around the previous night, and AC/DC's appearance at the record shop in particular. There, the band had sat at a long table and signed autographs for more than an hour, which delighted not only the fans but also the manager of the store, who witnessed a steady flow of album sales. Angus was presented with a makeshift electric chair to sit in, and the mood was relatively light-hearted until the young guitarist suddenly leapt up and engaged in a minor scuffle with one of the customers. Although quite small, Angus can be notoriously fearsome when roused, and on the bus he revealed what had happened.

'Well, I'd been sitting in that chair for quite a while, and this guy had been heckling me a bit,

but that didn't really bother me too much. Then he started to call me short—and I wasn't going to let anybody do that, so I began laying into him. Some things I can take—but calling me short is out the the question!'

Eventually we hit the outskirts of San Antonio, passing the Alamo on our way into the town.

> "They've let the animals out of their cages."

The venue was packed with fully-fledged headbangers, who found the line-up of AC/DC, Molly Hatchet and Riot entirely to their satisfaction. It was, without doubt, the heaviest audience I've ever seen, and when the doors were opened one roadie commented: 'That's it— they've let the animals out of their cages!' The metaphor was well-chosen.

Both Hatchet and Riot provided excellent sets,

but it wasn't until the houselights had dimmed prior to AC/DC's performance that the kids went really wild. San Antonio is one hell of a heavy metal city.

AC/DC kicked off with *Live Wire,* creating an electric atmosphere. Angus paced about the stage in his schoolboy gear, like an untamed baby bull let loose in the ring. Naturally enough, he and Bon attract most of the attention—but throughout the show it's impossible not to admire the sheer consistency of rhythm guitarist Malcolm Young, bassist Cliff Williams and drummer Phil Rudd.

The band now have an abundance of material from which to select a set, and during their 75 minutes on stage in San Antonio they blended songs from *Highway to Hell* with such standards as *Sin City, Let There Be Rock, Riff Raff,* and *The Jack.* Of the more recent material, *The Girl's Got Rhythm* and *Walk All Over You* were particularly effective.

One commendable point of the AC/DC live show is their minimal use of visual effects. Instead of a multitude of technicalities, the force of the band comes across primarily through the music.

Angus is fun to watch, and he still does his 'walkabout' into the audience during the show—although in San Antonio this feature was even more amusing than usual, since Molly Hatchet axeman Dave Llubeck donned shorts and cap and had three of his crew carry him out at the same time as Angus. The young Aussie had begun from the left hand side of the stage while Llubeck set out from the other. Eventually the two of them met face to face, with Angus still playing and his *doppelganger* miming.

As soon as the show ended, the band cooled-off backstage, and in no time at all their dressing room was packed, mainly with females. With no gig the following day, the partying went on through the night. Towards the end of it someone shouted: 'Bon's drunk poison!', and—blind drunk—the singer made a rapid break for the bathroom. I noticed that a bottle of after-shave was empty.

There was no sign of Bon again until 24 hours later, when the party reassembled to leave San

Antonio. Bon emerged with a mass of bruises, and it transpired that he'd spent the previous afternoon with members of Molly Hatchet on some nearby rapids. A secondary explanation for the bruises might have been provided by the appearance of a rather large lady with whom he'd just spent the night—which put me in mind of the words of *Whole Lotta Rosie,* one of the band's best songs where he sings, 'Wanna tell you a story, 'bout a girl I know... she ain't exactly pretty, ain't exactly small...'
(Steve Gett, November 1979)

The band live like the Mafia

As the acclaim given to AC/DC by the Americans continued to mount, a tremendous sense of impending climax affected the band generally, and though pleasurable, must have added to the overall stress of touring.

Their mounting success took them ever further from their roots in Sydney. Sylvie Simmons' adjective 'homeless', used to describe them, was accurate, even though they were seasoned tourers and accustomed to the touring lifestyle. Bon Scott told Phil Sutcliffe:

"None of us have had our own places to live for the past two years. I rented a flat for eight months but I was only there for six weeks. All we've got is our parents' homes in Australia. We live in hotels, and we don't say at the end of a gig, 'I'm goin' back to the hotel', we've got into the habit of sayin', 'I'm goin' home'."

Angus agreed: "The band live like the Mafia. Bon's always been of no fixed abode and I'm in the flat above. If you're really wealthy maybe you can afford to say 'Whammo, I'll have that block of apartments there. I suppose I'll buy a place some time but I'll probably end up with one of those police boxes at a city crossroads so I can be in the thick of it. At the moment I'm quite at home in these motels. I'll go to me parents at Christmas and after a week I'll check into a hotel. I mean I've got brothers who bring their kids round and at six in the mornin' they'll

This is for real

fuckin' jump on you yellin', 'He's home!' In a hotel I could complain about the noise and change the rooms." (What, young Angus complain about noise?!)

On world tours AC/DC often surround themselves with objects and customs that are familiar to them. At Christmas time, 1981, Brian Johnson described the backstage scenes to BBC Radio DJ Tommy Vance:

"...You've got the old dart board, in the bar. The great thing is when you go backstage first of all, and you're playin' darts, those 15,000 or 20,000 kids waitin' for you don't seem such a threat anymore. Because you're worryin' about getting through to the next round of the darts final... at 10 dollars a head, why that's 200 pounds. It's good because it makes it feel a little bit like home.

"We have an actual club backstage, which is called the Bell End Club. The crew's got to buy a membership ticket. All it is is just escapism. When the lads are on the road in America, the pace really does start crippling you, you start not being able to go to sleep until seven in the morning. Your whole life is just totally knocked on the head. Darts help you feel that you're still at home. We're just cheatin', just pretending. You snap out of it when the curtains open; you hear the crowd startin' to go crazy, you realize *this is for real.* All your little foibles, your little sayings that you say to each other before you go on, is all forgotten. And you've got to get down to some hard work."

The sense of mental dislocation long-distance travel causes must have been intense at times of emotional stress or depressions brought on by euphoria. Individually, the band have various levels of tolerance, Angus apparently thriving on repeating bouts of mayhem, and Phil Rudd losing himself in his hobby of model road racing, using a kit he freights about from gig to gig. Though more laid back publicly than Angus, Malcolm Young shares his brother's ability to pace himself. Cliff Williams is adaptative and self-contained. Bon Scott, however, coped with life in his usual 'existential' way. He was a marvellous 'responder'. His refuge was his usual one of drink and 'good time'. The very outwardness that enabled him to give so much of himself on stage, offstage, was often untight, wayward, sometimes hazardous.

Angus: "We were going from California to Austin, Texas, and we stopped off at Phoenix for fuel. We're just takin' off again when someone says, 'Where's Bon?' He'd followed this bird off the plane and we reckoned he'd drunk so much he wouldn't even know what country he was headed for..."

Bon Scott: "We'd been drinking in the airport bar for about 10 minutes when I says, 'Don't you think it's time we caught our plane?', and she says, 'What do you mean *our* plane? I'm staying here'. I runs back and the fuckin' flights gone. Anyway she takes me to this black bar— she was Mexican—and I starts drinkin' and playin' pool. I had a good night, beatin' every bastard. After about two hours playin' this big-titted black chick and beatin' her too, I happen to look around and the whole bar is goin' 'Grrrr'.
"I think, 'Uhoh Bon', gives her another game and lose 9-1. 'Anyone else want to beat me?' I says. So I escapes with me life, only barely—and I made it to the gig in Austin."

But the mass of empty bottles he saw later in the hotel suite belied the impression. During the course of the interview Bon ordered more drink by phone.

If you want blood you've got it!

Bon's way of coping meant that he was always taking an awful lot of damage. Steve Gett followed the band on their UK tour, and in his articles showed concern about the level of drinking shown by the singer. At a party thrown by Atlantic to celebrate the first of the year's sell-out concerts at London's Hammersmith Odeon, he witnessed 'huge quantities' of alcohol being consumed, especially by Bon, who needed to have his stomach pumped out before he could appear on stage. The previous week, in the band's rooms at the Swiss Cottage Holiday Inn, Gett noticed that Bon was looking in excellent health, and even caught himself hoping that the friendly Aussie-Scot had given up hard drink.

1979 certainly brought nothing other than Rock business hassles and ego frustrations to complain about, however. Sales of albums were increasing dramatically. The success of their new album was stimulating the sales of earlier ones. In June, IF YOU WANT BLOOD YOU'VE GOT IT was at the top of British reader polls.
As well as the HIGHWAY TO HELL album, a single, HIGHWAY TO HELL/ IF YOU WANT BLOOD YOU'VE GOT IT, taken from the album, was released simultaneously with the album. GIRLS GOT RHYTHM (the band's first and only EP) was released in October. Side One takes tracks from HIGHWAY TO HELL *(Girls Got Rhythm* and *If You Want Blood You've Got It),* and Side Two from the IF YOU WANT BLOOD YOU'VE GOT IT album *(Hell Ain't A Bad Place To Be* and *Rock'n'Roll Damnation).* A single, GIRLS GOT RHYTHM/GET IT HOT was released in the same month, both tracks taken from the album.

If the band had one big regret it was that the year's business had not enabled them to tour Australia, and they were worried that increasing fame (and its demands) were taking them away from their first and probably most loyal fans. Firstly, their move to Lange's Roundhouse had severed another link with their home country. Secondly, as usual, Australia's 'Establishment' rules (experienced now at a different and more pernicious level) were operating against them. Bon explained their difficulty:

We still need Australia

"We have a totally English crew now as well as an English bassist, and we couldn't get working visas for them over there. They've gone into the Australian Embassy in London, perhaps on a Monday morning, and seen somebody who's been knocked off by his wife the night before. When they explain they work for us, an Australian band, the guy has simply questioned why the group can't get better Australian roadies, crew and bass player. As a result they can't get the visas.

"The thing is we do still need Australia, and we continue to sell albums over there, although it's obviously not the most important market for us now."

Stick two fingers up at mediocrity

Success *was* the reason for their neglect. They could not turn back and tackle the problems of entering Australia just as they were on the eve of huge American success. But equally to blame was the small-mindedness of some Australian officials, part of a breed of mind unfortunately found world-wide (like the promoter who 'pulled the plug') which put considerations of labor, loyalty to country, conformity to regulations, 'sensibleness', and so forth, before the necessities of art and artistes, and think that there is no difference apart from circumstances between John Lennon and their son. They are human shit, and if there are signs that the music of AC/DC still has meaning (to stick two fingers

up at mediocrity and such low-lives who have
weasled their way to power), they are these
confrontations that the band continually have to
withstand.

During the fall and throughout the winter, until
February 1980, AC/DC's Rock'n'Roll ferocity
continued apace. The UK Highway To Hell tour
had started on October 25 at the Newcastle
Mayfair and ended on November 9 at Leicester's
De Montfort Hall. But a series of added
December dates at Brighton, London and
Birmingham, formed a second UK mini tour,
and between November 9 and the start of these
Christmas dates the band also made an extensive
tour of Europe.

Many of the UK gigs were double acts each
covering two consecutive nights. A record total
of five nights were played at the Hammersmith
Odeon in London, enjoyed by the still swelling
ranks of fans but not by one NME journalist,
Stuart Johnson:

**The music was ugly, and... the almost
exclusively male audience was the ugliest I've
seen outside of a Glasgow Rangers game. But...
do they like the music because they're ugly or do
they become ugly as a result of it?**

Whatever, it was a fascinating gig... and if a
**tarantula spider were to place itself in front of
me I wouldn't be able to take my eyes off that
either.**

**What this music has to do with Rock'n'Roll is
no longer even a question worth asking. It's
clearly a sub-culture on its own and its devotees
neither want nor deserve any better.**

During the lightning tour of Europe in
November, Bon Scott pulled a leg muscle which
became inflamed on the day the band were due
to play their Southampton UK date. The gig
subsequently was cancelled, but replayed on
January 27 1980, two days after a one-off gig at
Newcastle (on the 25). During this month
AC/DC also found time to attend the Midem
Festival in Cannes, where they were presented
with a Gold Disc for sales of IF YOU WANT
BLOOD YOU'VE GOT IT, and a Silver Disc
for HIGHWAY TO HELL, which had climbed
into the European Top Ten during the fall.

At the end of January, Atlantic released a new
single, TOUCH TOO MUCH. The title track is
taken from the HIGHWAY TO HELL album,
but the reverse side, which plays at 33⅓,
contains interesting live versions of songs
recorded during the fall tours, *Live Wire* and
Shot Down In Flames, and for those who like
such things is a small fortuitous record of Bon
Scott's voice in concert during his last months. 61

CHAPTER SEVEN

A TOUCH TOO MUCH is a sad, tragi-comic, inadvertently prophetic comment on the death of Bon Scott.

The singer died suddenly on Thursday February 21, 1980, at the age of 33, during the same year that was to claim the life of John Bonham, Led Zeppelin's drummer, who also died an alcoholic-related death. Like Bonham's his death didn't cause great culture shock among Rock society as had the death of Jim Morrison, Sid Vicious or Ian Curtis. It was in many ways an ignoble and sordid death that gave fuel to the anti-AC/DC elitist elements of the music press some of whom saw the death as the amusing come-uppance of a piece of risen Aussie dirt. But to the masses of fans, and to the band itself, it was a tremendous loss.

The first member of AC/DC to hear what had happened was Angus Young, who was phoned by the girlfriend of Alisdair Kinnear, a musician friend of Bon Scott and Bon's companion on the night of his death. Angus received the call on the evening of the 21.

"I immediately phoned Malcolm, because at the time I thought maybe she's got the wrong idea, you know, *thought* it was him. And Ian, our tour manager, said it couldn't be him 'cause he'd gone to bed early that night. Anyway, the girl gave me the hospital number, but they wouldn't give me any information until his family had been contacted. Anyhow, Malcolm rang Bon's parents 'cause we didn't want them to be just sitting there and suddenly it comes on the TV news, you know."

At first, I didn't really believe it

"Peter (Mensch, the band's British representative from Leber and Krebbs) got to the hospital as soon as he could, to find out exactly what had happened and identify him, because everyone was in doubt at the time. At first, I didn't really believe it, but in the morning it finally dawned on me."

It was too late to save the singer's life

The details gradually became clear to a shocked and confused band. The facts were not easy to believe for several reasons. Firstly, there was the sheer suddenness of Bon's death—when last seen by the band only hours beforehand, Bon had been in good health and enthusiasm for new recording work that they had embarked on. Secondly, the circumstances leading to his death were not out of the ordinary.

Bon had been with Kinnear at London's Music Machine club on the night of February 20. There, Kinnear claims, Bon consumed at least seven double whiskies (not a great deal by Bon's standards, even if the figure is rounded up). They left the club at 3.0 am. Then, in Kinnear's car on the short jouney home Bon became unconscious (again, not unusual; Bon often went to sleep after drinking). They reached Bon's flat, where Kinnear had arranged to leave Bon, but the singer proved difficult to rouse and couldn't easily be moved.

Anyone who has tried to awaken someone from such a sleep, let alone try to remind him or her of practicalities, will know how difficult it can be to draw a response. Kinnear therefore decided that the best course of action to take would be to put Bon up for the night at his own home, in East Dulwich, South East London. He drove there, but when they arrived Bon was still heavily asleep. He tried to lift Bon out of the car, but was unable to. He eventually decided that the best course of action would be to leave Bon in the car to 'sleep it off'. He got blankets, to make sure Bon was as comfortable as possible, locked the car doors for safety, and then went to bed to get some sleep himself.

Unfortunately, Bon was either left in (or moved into) a position that caused his neck to twist slightly. During his sleep be vomited, and choked.

Kinnear slept for about 15 hours, and it was early evening before he awoke. Checking Bon, he realized that something was wrong. In a panic he rushed him to London's King College Hospital, but by then it was too late to save the singer's life.

While Kinnear was traveling to the hospital, his girlfriend rang Angus to tell him that she thought Bon was dead. Angus immediately phoned the hospital, but because he was not Bon's next of kin, could get no confirmation. He then phoned Peter Mensch, who went to the hospital in person. Mensch managed to learn that Bon was in fact dead.

It was many weeks before the band could reorientate themselves. Because of the nature of Bon's death there had to be an inquest, and the band's presence was required at the court to give their version of the circumstances and to supply evidence and testimonies.

The coroner reported that Bon's stomach had been found to contain the 'equivalent of half a bottle of whiskey' at the moment of death. Peter Mensch told him that this was not unusual. Bon had always drunk a lot before and after performances, but this had not impaired his performance on stage. During 1979 the band had played 250 concerts, and Bon had sung on every occasion. When it was their turn to speak, the band said that they could only remember one occasion attributable possibly to drink when Bon couldn't sing at a gig, and that was when he had unintentionally got off an aeroplane in the wrong city.

"Captain of his own destiny"

Commenting that Bon's liver, kidneys and general health were excellent considering his reputation, the coroner recorded a verdict of Death by Misadventure. He added that Bon had been the "captain of his own destiny".

The suddenness of the tragedy completely halted the band's momentum. Prior to Bon's death they had started to record their seventh album since leaving Australia, and after the success of HIGHWAY TO HELL they had been in an extremely confident and buoyant mood about the prospects of recording their next. The improvement that had already taken place in Bon's vocals under Lange's supervision could be bettered, and many of the tracks intended for the new album had already been laid down in readiness for this.

Angus: "Malcolm and I were really looking forward to getting Bon in the studio; more than we'd done with any album before, because, after the success of the last one it was going to be a

AC/DC meets Blackfoot. Left to right: Jackson Spires, Greg T. Walker, Angus Young, Rick Medlocke, Malcolm Young, Charlie Hargrett

really big challenge, you know. *That* was the saddest part of it, 'cause it could perhaps have been the best thing he'd ever done on record. I think that's the real loss for everyone, especially the fans, 'cause they would've had a chance to hear him at his peak. That would have been the crowning glory of his life.

Instead, the band now had to attend to the immediate practical problems of the funeral, and flying Bon's body back to Australia and consoling his parents. After that would come the myriad question marks that had been raised about recording contracts, future engagements, and their future as a band. For the moment these considerations were kept in the background by Peter Mensch.

The band arrived back home in the country that had always made it difficult for them as performers, for a quiet funeral ceremony and memories of their first years together that must have made Angus, Malcolm and Phil in particular, unhappy and possibly bitter. But Angus turned this round:

Angus: "A lot of people sort of think it's sad for us—and it's true, it was just like losing a member of our own family, maybe even worse, because we all had a lot of respect for Bon as a person, 'cause, even though he did like to drink and have a bit of a crazy time, he was always there when you needed him to do his job, and I think in his whole career there's maybe only three shows he ever missed, and that was 'cause his voice wasn't there and we didn't really want him to sing. But I think it's more sad for the guy himself, you know, 'cause he always said he would never go unless he was famous. And *that's* sad for him because just as he was getting somewhere—he's been at it a lot longer than us, you know, he's been singing for something like 15 years—and it *was* sad for him in that way 'cause he really hadn't reached his peak."

Though a large number of fans turned up outside the chapel, the funeral itself was kept quiet out of consideration for Bon's family. After it was over, the band returned to England to try to think out their next move.

Tributes to Bon had started to appear almost immediately after Bon's death. Most of the British press devoted some space to him. Dave Lewis, who had been about to interview both

The best thing he'd ever done on record

Bon and Angus about their latest tours as well as the band's new single, A TOUCH TOO MUCH, wrote in Sounds (March 29) that Bon "seemed positively to revel in the classic Rock'n'Roll lifestyle. It was his escape route from the boredom of his small-time Australian upbringing where the general attitude was that anyone who tried to make a living out of music was just a shirking lay-about, and probably a pooftah".

And he quoted movingly from the lyrics of Bon's *Rock'n'Roll Singer:*

"'Well you can stick your nine-to-five living and your collar and tie,
And you can stick your moral standards 'cause it's all a dirty lie,
You can stick your golden handshakes and you can stick your silly rules
And all the other shit that you teach the kids at school,
'Cause I ain't no fool,
Gonna be a Rock'n'Roll singer
Gonna be a Rock'n'Roll singer'."

Atlantic were among the first to respond. A spokesman told the Record Mirror: "Bon's voice was very distinctive, and we have all suffered a great loss. During the three years that I knew him he was always helpful and willing to work hard for AC/DC and the record company. He made many friends and will be missed greatly".

But later in the year, in August, an Atlantic copywriter, in a press release, painted a more heroical picture:

Bon Scott was always the top joker in the AC/DC pack, almost ten years Angus' senior and a former roadie with the band. The stories of his sexual and alcoholic excesses are legion and that part of his enormous fan mail that didn't involve tempting offers from young girl fans invariably berated him for 'leading poor Angus astray'. Sadly, Bon is no longer with us after he tragically went just one step too far on

one of his notorious boozing binges. But if there is a crumb of comfort to be found in such a needless and premature death, it is that Bon probably went out the way he would have chosen, never flinching as he went over the top just one more time.''

''Never flinching as he went over the top just one more time''?? This seems to suggest that Bon might have derived *enjoyment* from dying, and I can only hope that those of us who share Bon's temperament don't take this too literally. Relatively Constant Copywriter: there can never be any heroism in a pointless death.

Brian Johnson, in conversation with radio DJ Tommy Vance after joining AC/DC, paid Bon a moving tribute:

''I think Bon Scott had a bit of genius. It annoys me that nobody recognized that before. He used to sing great words, write great words. He had a little twist in everything he said. Nobody ever recognized the man at the time. Oh great, when the man died they were startin' to say, 'Yeah, the man was a genius'. *That was too late,* too late; it's not fair. I think he was clever, so clever, and I think he had such a distinctive voice as well. He was brilliant.''

No blame was laid by the band on Bon's friend, Kinnear. Angus: ''I suppose he would feel worse about it, but possibly he thought he was doing the right thing at the time, 'cause he'd been out with Bon a few times, and Bon had done the same thing before.

''I've seen Bon on many occasions drink three bottles of bourbon straight off, and he could drink like that constantly. He was basically healthy; it was just the position he was in in the car that did it. Maybe if he'd been in a bad way he would've been okay, but you can't really say 'cause he could just have easily laid on his back or something and he would still have choked. It's a thing that could happen to anyone who drinks a bit or is sick for whatever reason.

''I've seen Bon fall asleep behind amplifiers. One moment he could be sitting watching TV and the next he would stand up, walk behind a couch and, bonk, fall over asleep. He was just like that; when he had a drink he could sleep anywhere, but he'd always be fine when he woke up in the morning. He would be up to three or four in the morning drinking his heart out, and then up again about 10 the next day to get a plane, and he was always a picture of health. He was remarkable.

In the form of interview, Angus himself paid many tributes to Bon, perhaps the best of which is the following. It shows the other side to the public image of Bon, and is the one which without doubt endeared him to the band and to his fans.

''Often Bon would trail off with fans who came backstage after a show and go off with them to a party or elsewhere. He judged people as they were and if they invited him somewhere and he was in the right mood to go, he went. It didn't matter to him whether they had a name or were a 'star', he just went with them. We used to call him 'Bon The Likeable'.

''We could be somewhere where you would never expect anyone to know him, and someone would walk up and say, 'Bon Scott!', and always have a bottle of beer for him. It was uncanny.

''One time we were broken down in a bus outside this little town in Australia and some guy came walking along with his surfboard and a whole crate of beer. And it was really hot and we were dying for a drink. Anyway, he walked by the bus and looked in, saw Bon and suddenly yelled, 'Bon Scott!', and came running in and handed out all his beers, and everyone was there for hours having a party while the bus was being fixed.

''He made a lot of friends everywhere and was always in contact with them, too. Weeks before Christmas he would have piles of cards and things, and he always wrote to everyone he knew, keeping them informed. Even his enemies, I think.'' (Chuckles). ''He certainly was a character.''

(Dave Lewis, ''The Show Must Go On'', Sounds, March 29)

━━━ CHAPTER EIGHT ━━━

"Do you wanna come back and rehearse"

"I thought, 'Well, fuck this, I'm not gonna sit around mopin' all fuckin' year'. So I just rang up Angus and said, 'Do you wanna come back and rehearse?'"
(Malcolm Young)

"We didn't really know what to do during the first few weeks after Bon's thing. It was as if we'd come so far and suddenly then what? But eventually Malcolm said that he and I were still writing and that we should really continue with it. There were a lot of commitments as well, a lot of people were dependent on us, so it seemed clear that we had to keep going."
(Angus Young)

AC/DC decided fairly quickly that they would not disband. Next to the band's and crew's livelihood, there were many wise reasons for this decision. A main consideration was the group itself. AC/DC was still growing; its members were still young and felt that they had not yet achieved the success of which they were capable; and as a unit the band still had a potent commercial image. A further consideration was the expectancy of the fans—they could not disband without letting down many of the people who had helped them in the past. Perhaps the over-riding concern, though, was Bon himself: while alive he would not have liked to have thought that his death would split the band. His heart and soul had been in AC/DC; it was as though the band had been his own life.

Malcolm, the band's original motivation, first vocalized the need to retain unity and keep up momentum, and rang Angus about two days after Bon's funeral to tell him what he thought. Angus agreed that to keep going was the only sensible course they could take. He told Dave Lewis:

"It's probably a lot better to keep working rather than just say 'stop', because then it becomes a lot harder and all you can do is think about something like that. So as soon as Malcolm and I came back from the funeral, we got straight back to work on the songs we'd been writing at the time it happened.

"The band will have to carry on now 'cause there's a lot of commitment for us... there's been no pressure put on us to keep going or anything, but as a band we decided to do it, though it's pretty hard at the moment to say what direction or whatever we'll take 'cause without Bon it was a unique thing. He *is* a unique character, and we wouldn't like to have someone there who was a Bon imitator. It would be better to get someone who's a bit unique in their own way. The band's music will probably stay the same, but the vocals will be a bit different. It's a very hard thing 'cause there's so many people with good voices, you know, and we're looking for something a little different. It's not like a guitar—you get pretty hoarse, so we've always let them try out when *they* feel right themselves, and to try and put them at ease. It's also difficult for any guy to walk in

67

knowing Bon's just died and probably thinking we're all going to be a bit funny about a new guy singing his songs.''

Lewis was interviewing the band at a rehearsal studio in South London where auditions were being held for a new singer. Four weeks after Bon's death he observed that the severe dent in the tightly-knit AC/DC family appeared to have healed—they had come to terms with the loss of their 'brother' and were treating Bon's death philosophically as just another of the many events that had happened to him.

The selection of the new singer was paramount among their immediate concerns, and there were many speculations about the replacement singer's identity. The Australian Press reported that AC/DC seemed likely to pick Stevie Wright, original singer with the Easybeats. Wright had left the Easybeats in 1970, apparently with a drug problem. He later spent 18 months in the musical, *Jesus Christ Superstar,* before recording two solo albums for Vanda and Young. When he was considered for the post of singer for AC/DC he was working as a drug councillor for the Salvation Army in Sydney.

Alan Friar, an Australian vocalist, was also on the shortlist. Friar was more or less informally selected, and was so confident of becoming AC/DC's new singer that he gave up his job in a local band. Then AC/DC's management (who had never been completely happy with Friar's lack of experience) diplomatically announced that a more experienced singer had been introduced to them on the last moment.

The 'experienced new' singer's arrival was a huge relief to Peter Mensch. The circumstances which led to his being hired constitute the second most oft-repeated story in Britain about the band (the first being the historic first gig at the Red Cow). The hiring was remarkable because it was brought about by the direct intervention of an AC/DC fan, and not by professional astuteness. Not many fans can lay claim to helping a top band at a crucial stage in their career. This fan not only provided AC/DC with a *singer;* he provided them with *the only* singer that could possibly replace Bon.

The fan was an American, from Chicago, who had read about the band's difficulties and thought that the solution might lie with a UK import album he had heard. He sent a tape of the album to Leber and Krebbs, and impressed on them the suitability of the album's vocalist. The tape was sent to Peter Mensch who, as it happened, liked the vocalist—and so did AC/DC. They were so impressed by the singer's voice, in fact, that they immediately started proceedings to track him down to find out whether he would like the job.

"I got this call from the band saying come down and look us over. I said, 'Listen, I can't spare much time, can we make it quick?' I did what they wanted and went back home and didn't think anymore about it, and then I heard I got the job. I owe that kid a great debt of gratitude.''

Brian Johnson's modest reaction to AC/DC's invitation to audition is typical. He was well aware that his future employers were a top band who had achieved far more success than he had with his own group, and he apparently did not assume that he stood even a remote chance of acceptance. He recalls, further, that he had been sitting at home after the audition when he was rung by an excited Malcolm. Malcolm did not tell him directly that he had got the job of singer. He told him first about a big win he'd just had on the horses (it was Grand National day), leading Brian to think the call was friendly and not particularly about business. Then Malcolm asked him to get down to London as quickly as possible because they had a great deal of work to catch up on. It suddenly dawned on Brian that he had been offered one of Rock's top jobs, and he dropped the phone.

Brian had done a good term as singer with 'Chant Rock' band Geordie—the band whose album had attracted the attention of the Chicago fan—and his voice was eminently suited to AC/DC's music. He has a voice uncannily like that of Bon's (without being a copy, which the band did not want), but with a unique power and expressiveness.

He was born in 1948, in Newcastle, UK, just inside England's border with Scotland. As a child he had appeared in TV plays, but his career turned musical and it was as a Rock singer with Geordie that he made his name. Geordie was disbanded when AC/DC approached Brian, but the group had struck a rich seam of gold in the Glam Rock era of the early 70s, in the wake of bands like Slade and T Rex, and had had a string of hits, including *Don't Do That, All Because Of You, Can You Do It* and *Electric Lady.* Abruptly, success faded, leaving Brian feeling depressed about the fickleness of the Rock world.

So much untapped talent in the North

"I was disillusioned with the Rock business. We were beginning to slog away at nothing—and there was a management deal I'd rather not talk about.

We used to buy music papers and see all these two-penny groups with stupid names getting wined and dined, while bands from the North East got ignored. There's so much untapped talent in the North which gets ignored by toffy-nosed Southerners.''

Like Angus and Malcolm though, Brian is a fighter. After disbanding Geordie he entered the vinyl car roofing business, and from there quietly resigned himself to a long and arduous battle to regain lost ground. When contacted by AC/DC he had been trying to reform Geordie, and had even contracted with the band's old management to do a solo album for them. The album, GEORDIE, was eventually released on the Red Bus label at the end of 1980. He also cut a single, TREAT HER LIKE A LADY/ROCKIN' WITH THE BOYS, which has now become a collector's item among AC/DC fans. But I doubt whether there was any serious mileage left in Geordie's sound, except on a small scale within the UK, and

69

the biggest boost to its reputation the band could have hoped to receive was from its casual 'association' through Brian with AC/DC.

Like a lot of the UK's Northern industrial towns with engineering and factory works, Heavy Rock music has always been well received in Newcastle. Geordie the band was named after the colloquial name given to Newcastle men—Geordies. Now Geordies are tough, and hard, and big drinkers. In Britain, the town has an identity as strong as a nation's. It has its own beer, and its own football team. The local dialect spoken there is so broad some would say that it also has its own language. But in international Rock terms it is best known for Eric Burdon and the Animals who, long before Geordie, started out on the club circuits of the North East in an attempt to make their name. The only other thing Newcastle is world-renowned for is that it is the birthplace of James Cawthorn, Britain's leading living fantasy illustrator.

Brian Johnson has a great deal of the Geordie character in his make-up—easy-going, earthy, no-nonsense, with a strong sense of competition...

Johnny Rotten's a wanker, and that's all there is to it

"I'm a Newcastle lad through and through, and I still want it to be my home. I suppose my career really started when I began listening to John Mayall and that Bluesy kind of stuff. I don't think I could call my voice beautiful, but at least it has guts. Heavy Metal has come back because I think it's honest, good time music. Punk and all that was just an image that ripped people off. Johnny Rotten's a wanker, and that's all there is to it."

...a character that seems to be personified in a chequered flat cap (a 'dut') tilted down over his forehead, which he is rarely seen without... definitely not, as he is quick to point out, an Elton John influence, but a barrier to keep the sweat out of his eyes on stage.

His energy and experience made him an active component of AC/DC from the moment he joined, and his level-headedness and friendliness squashed any early fears that he might not be able to 'fit in'. The only possible obstacle to his full acceptance might have been the fans, but given his genuine talents and sincere intentions this possibility seemed remote.

Angus had sufficient faith in him to tell him that his days in the second-hand car trade were over for good, and further that he was not to regard himself as the band's singer but as a full fifth member of the band. He should contribute in whatever way he could, even though he might feel that some of his ideas were too bold. Work on the new album benefited immediately from this approach, with Brian writing most of the eight songs. But Brian himself was most keen to get on the road, where he knew that he could repay the faith that had been put in him.

CHAPTER NINE

Life on the road

To AC/DC life on the road basically equals life itself. It is in the constant blur of planes, limos, hotel rooms, sound checks and shows that they thrive best, working (and playing) in an almost family atmosphere, band and roadcrew alike, that is both rare and contagious. And it is on the road where new vocalist Brian Johnson will finally earn his wings as a fully-fledged AC/DC, both in the band's eyes and, hopefully, yours. Already, his earthy and uproarious North Eastern humor has made him a favorite with everyone connected with the band—and they are even beginning to understand the thick Geordie accent that pours in a torrent from beneath his battered flat cap! But onstage the empathy between Brian and his new colleagues is total, his powerful Rock'n'Roll scream a perfect match to AC/DC's Heavy Metal maelstrom.
(Atlantic Press Release, August 1981)

"The first time I seriously sang with the band everybody just stood there open-mouthed. It was a very unusual experience for them because they'd been with Bon for so long. But I've settled in really well because they're all so friendly and hard working.

"This is the type of band I should have been with years ago. I can now see that I've been wasting a lot of time during my life. What I really like about the band is that they have no pretensions, they're just four ordinary blokes. When I was with Geordie you had to teeter around on stack heels and I never liked that."

"We haven't had too many language problems at the moment. Maybe just a few when I talk too fast; but otherwise they seem to understand every word I say."

"I'd got so used to having Bon there. But Brian's an individual, and that's helped a great deal, because he's a pretty natural person. Sometimes Bon would tend to pull back a bit more, and then come forward at others. Brian's very much like me—he's got a lot of energy and he's always up front."
(Angus Young)

"I remember not so long ago with Geordie we used to play this big club at the top of Gateshead (Newcastle), and I used to think it was really big-time when we'd get 900 people packed in there. Then the next thing I know I'm on the road with these lads, and Philadelphia was one of the first gigs we played. And the first night I walked out in front of all these yelling kids I thought, 'Hey, hang on a minute here, this isn't right'. I'm used to being a legend in my own lunchtime, not my bleedin' life!"

Before the band could commence touring they had to complete work on their new album. They had to work fast, to make up for lost time, with Brian virtually writing the songs straight on to the music. After they finished composing they began a schedule of rigorous rehearsals, working for seven hours each day until mid-April, when they were ready to record.

Success had brought new kinds of money considerations that were beginning to influence the way they lived as well as their whole working procedure. Getting hold of money was no longer such a problem; holding on to it, was. Therefore *where* they did their recording had become of strategic financial importance. Recording the new record in Britain would mean that they would have to pay Britain's high taxes. Like the Bee Gees, Fleetwood Mac and other bands before them they moved their base away from Britain (and the Roundhouse) to the Bahamas, and to Compass Point Studios.

Angus: "There were a lot of different reasons for us finally deciding to work out there. Tax was one of them, and another was the actual availability of studios. We wanted somewhere in England because the country has a great working atmosphere. We didn't really want to go over to Europe since most of the stuff from there tends to be Disco. There was one in Sweden that Zeppelin used, but that belongs to Abba, and at that point they themselves were using it. But we didn't want to hang around waiting, we just wanted to get on with it.

The extra troubles were rewarded

"It's actually very slow at Compass Point. I mean the studio itself is really very good, but the life style is such that you tend to spend half the day lying around on the beach and having to work at night. But we didn't do that. Once we start working we want to get on with it."

For a long time the new album had no title, a dilemma caused by the band's wish to ensure that its packaging properly reflected their feelings after their period of mourning. It was eventually titled BACK IN BLACK.

Angus: "Obviously we called the album BACK IN BLACK because of Bon. We didn't want to just say, 'Dedicated to Bon', because the guy had been with us for five years, and so we all decided that it was a far better tribute to him to design the whole album to him rather than just have one little line on the back of the sleeve."

BACK IN BLACK was recorded during April and throughout May, over a period of six weeks. Holdups in the transportation of the band's equipment from England had turned the task into more of an ordeal than they thought, but the extra troubles were rewarded spectacularly when the album was eventually released at the end of July.

The improved quality of the music, the new vocals, the band's persistence in keeping together, the new world tours, served to make BACK IN BLACK the album that immediately put AC/DC among the world's top Heavy Rock acts.

Reviews were mixed, with the sympathetic camp generally in agreement that the tracks were the best the band had released, especially *Hells Bells,* which was destined to become a new AC/DC classic. Most reviewers also agreed that Brian's vocals, similar to Bon's but higher-pitched, fitted nicely with the AC/DC sound. One reviewer thought that Angus had progressed from the solos of *High Voltage* to becoming a guitarist with *taste*. The 'anti-' camp dismissed the record (as was to be expected) as a 'tasteless cash-in', deliberately misinterpreting the album's point.

The album reached the top of the UK LP charts during the week of August 9, where it stayed for two weeks. In the US it reached number four during the week of January 17, 1981. Initially it sold about 12,000,000 copies, and its success (and the subsequent tours) ultimately brought fresh vitality to earlier albums. A re-released DIRTY DEEDS DONE DIRT CHEAP, on May 23, 1981, rose from virtual anonymity to number three in the US charts, years after its original release.

AC/DC did not hear concrete news of their UK success until they were on tour in America (in Norfolk, Virginia), and did not know the full extent of their American successes until they had returned to tour in Britain and then returned again to the States at the end of 1980.

Like the Highway to Hell World Tour, the Back in Black tour was undertaken on a large scale, and started in the US on July 30, at the County Fieldhouse, Erie, Pennsylvania. The tour, and follow-up tours that utilized its main features continued through 1980 and well into 1981, covering the UK, Europe, Japan and (after a long absence) Australia, as well as extra sojourns in North America.

America at last wholeheartedly had decided to accept the hard-working band, and from July to September AC/DC made their biggest-ever impact there, with audiences doubling-up on those of their last tour and with the airways busy with replays of AC/DC numbers.

For the first time the show included spectacle, in the form of a huge bell made of bronze and 'embossed' on its side with the AC/DC motif. The bell had been specially cast to augment Angus's guitar, and was featured at the start of each show. It was so heavy it had to

be winched down to stage-level by crane. Once lowered, it was struck with a large wooden mallet by Brian who sounded out a series of funereal chimes in dedication to Bon.

They had not easily taken to the idea of the bell because its inclusion went against what had been until then their most sacrosanct policy— not to include spectacle of any kind in their sets. But they wanted the new stage show, like the album, to incorporate a strong element of tribute. Playing taped bell chimes over a recording would not have appeared sufficiently substantial.

'Spectacle' had been introduced to AC/DC's act at the right time. On both the Back in Black 'Hell's Bells' tour, and their most recent tour, its presence has certainly enhanced the band's act in a big way. The addition has not detracted from the musical emphasis, as feared; if anything it has increased musical impact, for long gone are the days when AC/DC needed to prove that they could perform as opposed to mimick, or mask incompetence with special effects.

Their third gig of the tour, on August 1 at the Palladium, New York, was one of the most prestigious. Once the great Hell's bell had been lowered and struck, and its majestic, doom-laden sound had permeated around the auditorium, the band erupted into BACK IN BLACK'S opening track. There was no restraint: respect for Bon did not mean repression; it meant going over the top and having a ball. AC/DC were in black, but they were very definitely *back*.

Jim Farber of Sounds, and Steve Gett of Melody Maker both covered the show. Farber, in a sardonic (but not sarcastic) write-up, declared that because AC/DC were totally unpretentious and didn't try to come across as sex symbols (Van Halen), they were "Literally lightyears ahead of other HM bands". And they were, he continued, "perhaps the only band in the world with a guitarist who can moon at the audience and have it come off as utterly charming". Listening to AC/DC was like watching someone pick their nose for an hour-and-a-half. For Heavy Metal, this is no small compliment".

Steve Gett thought that Brian Johnson, clad in T-shirt, jeans and cap, delivered with consistent power, and noticed that he moved around more than Bon had done, giving the band added dimension. The band were more aggressive than ever. Their music, especially the rhythm work of Malcolm, Phil Rudd and Cliff Williams, which was "tighter than a clenched fist", had improved considerably. Notwithstanding Bon Scott's contributions, he sensed that this was AC/DC's moment. They were on the verge of great and dizzying heights.

They just want to touch the guitar

At the Milwaukee Auditorium, Wisconsin, David Fricke (Rolling Stone, October 30) noticed that Angus Young was carried on a roadie's shoulders now that Bon was no longer there to perform the ritual. This year dressed in green velvet uniform and striped tie (a further concession to the changing times), he was carried through the grasping, waving arms of the audience, flailing away on his guitar.

Brian sometimes continued Bon's role on the walk-abouts, but often preferred to sing and keep to the stage. Possibly he is nervous of getting into such direct contact with the crowd, possibly he just doesn't have that 'madman'

enjoyment to rampage possessed by Bon. But, according to Angus, although these little forays into the crowd are by no means as easy as they look, there has been little harm done by the crowd to him or to whoever carries him when he goes out.

"The kids really get into it and sometimes get over-excited, but they wouldn't really harm you. They just want to touch the guitar or hit a string. I've never really been harmed since I started doing it. I've had a few scraps and I've bopped a few people and a few people have bopped me, but that's all. I do get aggro from the bouncers though. I've been sitting on Plug's shoulders playing away, and bouncers have refused to let us through."

Ironically, it is with the concert and security guards who have been paid to keep order and protect the band, that AC/DC receive the most trouble. For the first time they found that they had to hire their own security 'heavies' to deal with the threats.

Angus: "We end up fighting with the guards, 'cause they won't believe we are the band. I don't ever listen to those kind of people. I just tell 'em to get out of the way, and we end up in a full-scale brawl while people are waiting for us to get back on stage, you know. (Laughs). That's why we got John and Wally."

Malcolm: "We got Wally and John around 'cause we've got a tendency as a band to get into trouble 'cause we've got such quick tempers. If we were easy-going people we could probably get to the gig in a taxi and persuade the security people to let us in 'cause we were the band, and so on. But because we're so snappy we would get the shit kicked out of us every night just trying to get *into* our own gigs. So that's really why we go to gigs in limos with these guys around us. They look after all that shit for us. I don't think any bastard knows who I am anyway, you know, but having them can have its advantages."

The British tour started at the Colston Hall, Bristol, on October 19, where Fred Williams of the Record Mirror, caught the band. The tour ended with the traditional three nights at the London Apollo, on November 14-16.

Bells toll in black before the band begin, and that's about the only memory of Bon Scott allowed. From here on in, it's a trip to the edges of insanity, conducted by vocalist Brian Johnson lurching around like a punch-drunk sailor. Angus Young not so much gripping his guitar as gripped by it, moving around in a fit of demented hysteria in which the only function he's capable of is playing his guitar.

Leaving that aside for a moment, it seems that the whole schoolboy element of AC/DC has passed its exams and left school; the bass and rhythm guitarists trot forward in step to sing harmonies, the audience respond to fist-raising gestures with perfect co-ordination, and even the school uniform has become a stylized green velvet, and from the way he walks, those shorts must have been squeaky tight.

Music as a socially cohesive force

Fortunately, the music is strong enough to have survived the showbiz spectacle and present a solid front of aggressive masculinity in which the rhythms are elegant structures from the heart of Heavy Rock, with the added bonus of more than three chords. Furthermore, the band use every trick in the book to maintain and extend the pre-climax tension; in *Barefoot Boogie,* Angus discards the suit and briefly bares his bum to the audience who, well, seem to like it. True worship.

High Mountains sees the climax, when Angus is carried around the balcony like an emperor, without missing a note of his solo. It's his show, and he doesn't blow it. Anybody doubting the power of music as a socially cohesive force should see an AC/DC show—the band were magnificent, but I'd give just as many stars to the crowd.

The bell could not be used at every venue on account of its size. To Brian's dismay it was too big to be used at his first gig with AC/DC in his home town of Newcastle, on October 4 and 5, and an alternative format had to be used there as at other gigs.

Equipment used on the UK tour (which was sold out before it started) was as follows: Angus Young—two Gibson SGs, two radio transmitters, three Marshall 100 watt stacks; Malcolm Young—a Gretsch Falcon, a Gretsch Rock Jet, three Marshall 100 watt stacks, one Marshall 50 watt combo; Cliff Williams—a Fender Precision, a Fender Jazz, three Marshall 8 × 10s, three Ampeg SVTs; Phil Rudd—a sonor custom kit, Zildjian cymbals; Brian Johnson—the one ton bronze bell.

Brian's first two tours with AC/DC finished in personal triumph. He had been overwhelmingly accepted by the fans and had more than amply fulfilled his pledge to prove his worth on the road. But it had not been without a battle against the pessimism and hostility of some of the music press, and his own doubts and fears, and sometimes it had been an eerie and emotional experience, as he recounted earlier that year at Compass Point to Dave Lewis who asked him how it felt to occupy Bon's shoes:

"All I can really say is that Bon is still around and watching. I can't tell you anymore because it's all so personal. But at night in my hotel room I had proof that he was there in some form. I know that he approves of what the new line up is trying to do. He didn't want the band to split up or go into a long period of mourning. He wanted us to build on the spirit he left behind.

"It's strange how Rock music breeds ecstasy and tragedy. You build up that great feeling every night when you go on stage and then suddenly death strikes in the strangest form.

The truth of the matter was that Bon died because he vomited when his neck was twisted and he choked. Had somebody been there in the car with him then it might have been a different story. It's the kind of freak accident that happens to people every day. Because he was a star the story becomes inflated.

That poor boy was loved by thousands of people worldwide. When we did a warm up gig in Holland this kid came up to me with a tattoo of Bon on his arm and said, 'This bloke was my hero but now he's gone. I wish you all the luck in the world'. I just stood there shaking, I mean what can you say when people are prepared to put their faith in you like that? Since then I feel like I've been singing for that kid and so many others like him. I hope that I've been accepted by AC/DC fans. They want the band to go on as well, and certainly I've had no letters or phone calls saying 'get out'."

CHAPTER TEN

As well as BACK IN BLACK and TOUCH TOO MUCH, there were two other releases in 1980, both singles and both taken from BACK IN BLACK. YOU SHOOK ME ALL NIGHT LONG/HAVE A DRINK ON ME, was released in August and rose to number 20 in the UK national singles charts. This was not a brilliant showing if AC/DC were a 'singles' band. But apart from LET'S GET IT UP (which *did* threaten to transform the band in this way early in 1982 when it reached number nine in the charts probably on account of its suggestive lyric as much as the band's stature), the band has retained its 'purity'. AC/DC wouldn't and probably couldn't have it any other way:

Angus: "We've sold lots of records by touring, 'cause we never used to get much airplay. Even BACK IN BLACK never got that much exposure, and they often stick us on in the early hours of the morning when they think no one will be listening.

"I don't think you could ever think of us as a big hit singles band. We'd have to bend with the wind, like the Stones do, unless we could come up with the ultimate Rock single, but they're few and far between.

"And whenever anyone suggests using this song or that song as a single I just cringe at the thought, 'cause I think the UK show Top of the Pops and those kind of shows are shit, and I just can't see us competing with the likes of Des O'Connor to get on them."

But someone, somewhere in Atlantic, doesn't quite agree with this point of view, and another single, ROCK AND ROLL AIN'T NOISE POLLUTION/HELLS BELLS, was released in November. It did better, reaching number 15, and was available both as a 7″ and a special collector's 12″ edition.

AC/DC's business muscles

The end of 1980 also saw the release of GEORDIE, the Red Bus album featuring Brian's vocals—which turned out to be a dated album, save for two tracks, *Rockin' With The Boys* and *Going Down*—and is interesting primarily because of the vocals.

AC/DC's business muscles tensed in other areas, and press reports and announcements were starting to show an increased sensitivity about matters of 'piracy'. In December 1980, display adverts appeared in the press warning fans not to deal with bogus fan clubs or purchase AC/DC merchandise except through official channels. Merchandise purchased *outside* venues or through unofficial mail order was likely to be substandard.

Then in July 1981 came reports that AC/DC had apparently become worried about the erosion of sales by album taping.

The latest concern had been triggered by the practice of blank tape marketing company '3M' of using freebie AC/DC badges to promote sales. A spokesman for (apparently) AC/DC themselves was reported as saying: "AC/DC regard home taping as potentially fatal to the record industry, and 3M's sales campaign is a cynical attempt to link AC/DC with Scotch tape. We are consulting our lawyers".

It is not easy in cases like this to know whether the band, their record company or both are vocalizing the fears. Certainly, when it comes to the practice of bootlegging (as opposed to copying or pirating records) it is the record companies who are talking, supported only in certain cases by the bands themselves. Quite often bands support bootlegging, and I know of at least two bands who have come forward to apologize to parties injured by record companies who have prosecuted in the band's names. To the artist, as opposed to the accountant, bootlegging can be highly desirable. It acts as a gentle nudge to record manufacturing to make material available

The BPI's overblown 'Operation Moonbeam' campaign

to their fans, and it also keeps records of concerts and media appearances which might otherwise be lost forever. More dubiously (to the artist but not to the fan) it ensures that second quality material—and therefore a part of the nature of the bands concerned—may also be preserved for posterity.

The attitude of record companies and artists to copying and pirating, either records or merchandise, is far more justifiable, and I would not expect many bands to allow the practice of either if they had the choice. In the realm of album taping, sadly for them, that choice is probably not available. In Britain, the British Phonograph Industry (BPI), scourge of bootleggers, piraters and copyers alike, and an 'umbrella' company which collectively represents the record companies' rights and theoretically (by association) the bands themselves, tried for much of 1981 to get a levy slapped on the sale of blank tapes. The company ran into serious obstacles, not the least being that to impose a realistic levy of say $2 on each blank tape would in many cases be to make that blank tape more expensive than a pre-recorded one. Another British organization, the Association of Professional Recording Studios (APRS), who supported the levy idea, also pointed out that companies could get round the levy, were it imposed, by recording non-copyright music or even a series of electronic bleeps on to cassettes intended for sale for use as blank tapes; such 'pre-recorded' tapes, not being blank, could not legally be subjected to levies, and therefore could be marketed at a low price not much higher than that of blank tapes.

Pirates and copyers

But looked at from the public's point of view, it is probably just as well that a way of enforcing a levy has not yet been found, for if the highly questionable methods used by the BPI to stop bootlegging were allowed to be used against companies and individuals who commit 'infringements' with ordinary cassette tapes, Britain at least would take a further strong lurch toward a form of commercial fascism imposed by so-called 'free' enterprise. In the BPI's overblown 'Operation Moonbeam' campaign first mounted in 1979 to bust a 'syndicate' of bootleggers operating within Britain, their agents colluded in the alleged manufacture of albums in order to obtain convictions. Strong-arm, gangster-type tactics like this, done within the law, are still being

used, with the 'syndicates' often turning out to be small fry fans (who may subsequently face huge, inproportional fines) who are 'in to' the bands they are bootlegging.

If there was a sign (to British fans at least) that AC/DC had almost 'made it' it was the band's absence from Britain during much of 1981—just as their absence from Australia during 1979 and 1980 had indicated the same to Australian fans. It was not simply their absence, but their *presence in absence,* in the all-pervasive form of record and press releases, films, merchandizing and reader polls, that gave rise among fans to such a feeling.

In February, BACK IN BLACK was polled second in the album section of Sound's Heavy Metal Reader's Poll (Motorhead's ACE OF SPADES was voted top). Angus Young was voted third best guitarist behind Ritchie Blackmore (top) and Michael Schenker (second). AC/DC were beaten to 'Top Band' by the swiftly-risen Motorhead. And readers of Kerrang!', the new British magazine for Heavy Metal devotees launched by Sounds, had just voted BACK IN BLACK number four in its 'All Time Top 100 Albums'.

In June the band featured (on celluloid) in the British 'Sounds Atomic Rock Show' which started on June 17 and ran until July 10, touring 24 towns. The show was a mixture of film previews and live acts, headlined by a very live More, and including film of AC/DC, Blackfoot

and Foreigner. Prizes and give-aways there were aplenty, including, to a lucky few, tickets to the forthcoming 'Monsters of Rock' Donnington Castle festival on August 8—where AC/DC *were* to make an appearance, their first and only British appearance of the year.

Castle Donnington, formerly a haunt for bikers and Hell's Angels, and a good race track, had become a legend to Heavy Rock fans after only one performance there by Heavy bands the previous year. The bill of 'Monsters' that year included Rainbow, Judas Priest, Scorpions and Saxon. The highlight of the show were Rainbow, who had announced previously that this was to be their farewell gig, to allow Ritchie Blackmore (one rumor went) to reform Deep Purple. Intent therefore on making a spectacular exit, during their set Rainbow's special effects team detonated a pile of gelignite, causing mayhem, much equipment damage and damage to eardrums.

This year's festivities had AC/DC at the top of a bill featuring Blue Oyster Cult, Whitesnake, Slade, More, Blackfoot and DJ Tommy Vance, and drew crowds far in excess of the numbers anticipated by the organizers. But though the festival was to be a great success in most respects, in one big respect, for AC/DC, it was not. The band suffered badly from sound problems, and in a year when their reputation was high and they were expected to perform as superstars, they were seen to be upstaged by several of the support bands. They had been well received in Japan, Europe and (after many years absence) in Australia, where they had played at one venue to an ecstatic audiencce of over 100,000, and the timing of the flawed Donnington performance came as a great misfortune.

Part of the sound problems AC/DC experienced stemmed from the large crowd. Malcolm Hill Associates, (who were handling the PA), and AC/DC themselves, took along equipment for a crowd of only 45,000-50,000, when more like 80,000 turned up, so bands that had brought more powerful equipment played to better effect. In addition, damp had got into the PA system and started to affect amplification during the AC/DC set. Hardest hit were the fans, among whom were a great many in the middle and at the back of the crowd who could hear AC/DC only partially well or hardly at all.

AC/DC did not realize the full extent of the sound loss until long afterward, and for them, ironically, the performance was an enjoyable and very welcome break from recording. They had started to record their new album FOR THOSE ABOUT TO ROCK, in July, and were experiencing certain difficulties, so the gig afforded them an opportunity to loosen up.

1981's most significant event was the recording and release (at the end of the year) of FOR THOSE ABOUT TO ROCK. As the band's success had grown, each album had taken progressively more out of them as they struggled to meet the higher standards they had set themselves, and this album was no exception. Mutt Lange was unhappy about the musical 'feel' they were achieving at new studios in Paris. Brian Johnson, interviewed at the beginning of 1982, reflected (Simon Tebbutt, Record Mirror):

"Some real power chords"

"I was dead pleased with FOR THOSE ABOUT TO ROCK, because on this album, unlike BACK IN BLACK, which was composed in such a rush Angus and Malcolm really took their time. We'd toured constantly for nearly a year and a half, and everybody just wanted a rest. Malcolm and Angus got the riffs together, and I met with them in Paris and we spent about three weeks rehearsing in an old factory outside Paris, and then Mutt came over and we went to the studios.

"But then we suffered a real setback. We just couldn't get the sound together in the studio. It wasn't the live sound we wanted. So we moved to another studio, just as we had to go to Donnington. In the end we just reverted to using the old factory that we'd rehearsed in, and it was a great sound there. We were really pleased with it, you know. Angus and Malcolm wanted to try some real power chords on this album, and I think it came off, real brilliant. There are some really classic tracks on there."

The factory needed equipping, and for this purpose it was eventually decided to invite over a British mobile studio. Recording finished in a week, enabling the album to keep more or less on schedule.

In the US, BACK IN BLACK had finally gone platinum. FOR THOSE ABOUT TO ROCK (WE SALUTE YOU) went platinum barely two months after its release.

CHAPTER ELEVEN

His mighty Thor hammer

The lights dim and the gig opens to the funereal chimes of the now famous Hell's Bell and the eruption of myriad tiny flames from matches and lighters held aloft by the audience. The bell is slowly lowered over the stage to head height, as Brian Johnson leaps onstage, strikes the bell four times with his mighty Thor hammer, and the band explode into *Shot Down In Flames.*

The venue: Spectum Ice Hockey Stadium, Philadelphia. The date: December 1981. It is number 22 on AC/DC's tour of the USA and Canada, which has been winding its way inexorably across the North American continent since the fall. They are packing in 20,000 punters a night—often three nights in a row in the same town.

Earlier in the tour, in Indianapolis, AC/DC played to an audience that had more than quadrupled since their last appearance there less than a year ago.

Brian: "We've been great on this tour. All the gigs have sold out, real big places too. Last time we played Indianapolis—last year, and I'd just joined the band—we played to about 4,000. Tonight what is there? 17,000? And they're brand-new audiences we're playing."

It is part-way on a tremendous, triumphant tour for AC/DC. In polls round the world for 1981 the band have come out on top, and they are at the moment indisputedly the world's top touring and grossing band barring the Rolling Stones.

Much is changing or has changed: Peter Mensch has been replaced by Ian Jeffery (AC/DC's former tour manager); Brian Johnson is making plans to move out of his little house in Newcastle to live abroad; Malcolm Young lives back home in Sydney; Cliff Williams lives in Hawaii; the band have an important new member—'The Boff'—to look after and design the electronics; Angus Young is wearing a *red* velvet school uniform; all of the band except Phil Rudd are now married. But the *essentials,* the essentials have not changed. Dave Lewis (Sounds, January):

A lewd, penis-like gesture

If anything, Angus seems to be laying on the wild-boy theatrics even thicker these days, writhing epileptically in a heap of thrashing arms and legs on the floor, dashing all over the stage and even up on the speaker stacks at one point, and during *Bad Boy Boogie* peeling off his tie, jacket and shirt and doing a bump'n'grind stroll along the front row of clutching hands, twirling his clothes in the air like a bullfighter's cape and catching the arm of his shirt between his legs in a lewd, penis-like gesture.

He also cheekily offers to take off his shorts too, sticking his fingers through his fly and finally mooning bare-assed from the drum riser as the band crash back into the riff.

The Spectum promoter has allowed the match and lighter flares, but fire regulations prevent AC/DC's newest danger to Mankind—a volley of cannon-fire set off at the end of the show as a salutation to the crowd. Instead of firing, the cannons—21 in all—have been adapted to spit sparks and smoke. A specially programmed

Prophet synthesizer (operated by Ian Jeffery) produces the sound of the thunderous explosions.

But fame has not altered the basic, non-hierarchical, AC/DC 'family' structure of band and crew. If anything, on tour, it has brought them even more tightly together, and they are more efficient at protecting their privacy. The clan amity extends outwards from this nub only very selectively—thus the few trusted journalists, and 'court' photographer, Robert Ellis (who has assembled a large and very comprehensive photographic archive of the band).

There are reservations, though—on Malcolm's part about the increasing tendency to use spectacle.

But the cannons, innocuous as they are, bring rocks on to AC/DC's collective heads. Just like almost everything else they do, the cannons manage to get up someone's nose—and that must surely be all to the good. AC/DC are the first band to take 'artillery' on the road, and in Hartford, Connecticut, they almost get thrown in jail. The fire marshals had complained to the police and the police were waiting for the band when they came offstage. Brian: "They had their handcuffs out ready for us and all that shit. They'd already clapped the cuffs on Ian in fact, and had a gun on his face threatening to stick us all in jail for a year for conspiracy to cause an explosion, or something. Crazy!"

In spite of the changes, fame has not altered the group's approach to their music, or their need to perform for their fans. World status may make AC/DC more inaccessible in some ways but in compensation it gives their fans a greater sense of individuality and importance. Beneath the cannons, the bells and the light shows, is still a hard-working Sydney club band, keeping a very tight control.

CHAPTER TWELVE

"When you're touring so much it's hard to prevent yourself getting stale. So I like to think bad. MEAN. Think mean, play mean. We like to get the tension up really high and leave it there. Townshend is always violent on stage. He must feel that way to look it and carry it off every time.

"Sometimes, when I've been playing particularly mean I have to be guided back to my dressing room because I can't see where I'm going.

So I dropped my trousers

When I'm on stage I'll think of anything to keep going. The kids in the audience have come to see you do something wild. They always want to see you better than the last time they saw you.

"We were playing the Reading Festival in '76 when all of a sudden this girl with enormous tits walked past the stage at the front. Everything seemed to stop as the whole mesmerized crowd watched this massive pair wander past. There was only one thing I could do in reply to that. So I dropped my trousers.

"I don't know why I do it. I just *do not* know. I think it might be 'cause of the drums, you know. It's always when I hear those drums pounding away. I mean, I've walked on stage and said to everyone, 'I am not going to do it', and Bam, I end up doing it. It's a weird thing. But we've got a lot more women in the audience this year. I don't know why...

"But whether I do it depends as well on how up the audience is, and I used to have more fun doing it to people who never knew what was going to happen. The good thing is that it does take away a lot of the serious side to the show 'cause people can have a laugh at it. I mean, I can't imagine Mick Jagger or someone like that doing it."
Angus Young

I have not written much, until now, about AC/DC's attitude towards music and life, and the way that this relates to their success, except to say that they are a Rock'n'Roll band in the true sense.

But what is Rock'n'Roll? In my book—and, I believe, in AC/DC's—Rock'n'Roll is about honesty, rebellion, and escape (having 'fun', which AC/DC constantly say they aim to do, can be got from these). Basic to all three is *honesty.* There is a saying that goes, 'never trust a man who can't dance'. The fact that a man cannot dance could preclude him from being a Rocker, and from honesty too, because on an orgastic dance floor it is difficult to hide feelings of insincerity towards one's fellow beings. If one is insincere he is forgetting he (or she) is an ordinary member of the people, and therefore is disqualified from making or appreciating Rock'n'Roll music. These are my words, and not the band's, but I think they explain why honesty of intent is a fundamental Number One AC/DC rule.

Angus: "I don't think I could walk on that stage and do what I do or any of the lads do if we couldn't be honest. If it all went bad, we would feel it more than anyone. I couldn't get out there and rip people off in any shape or form. If there's one thing I believe in then it's that. If you're not going to be honest in what you do, then you might as well fucking give up.

"There's no way you can hide it. Why try to hide what you really are?"

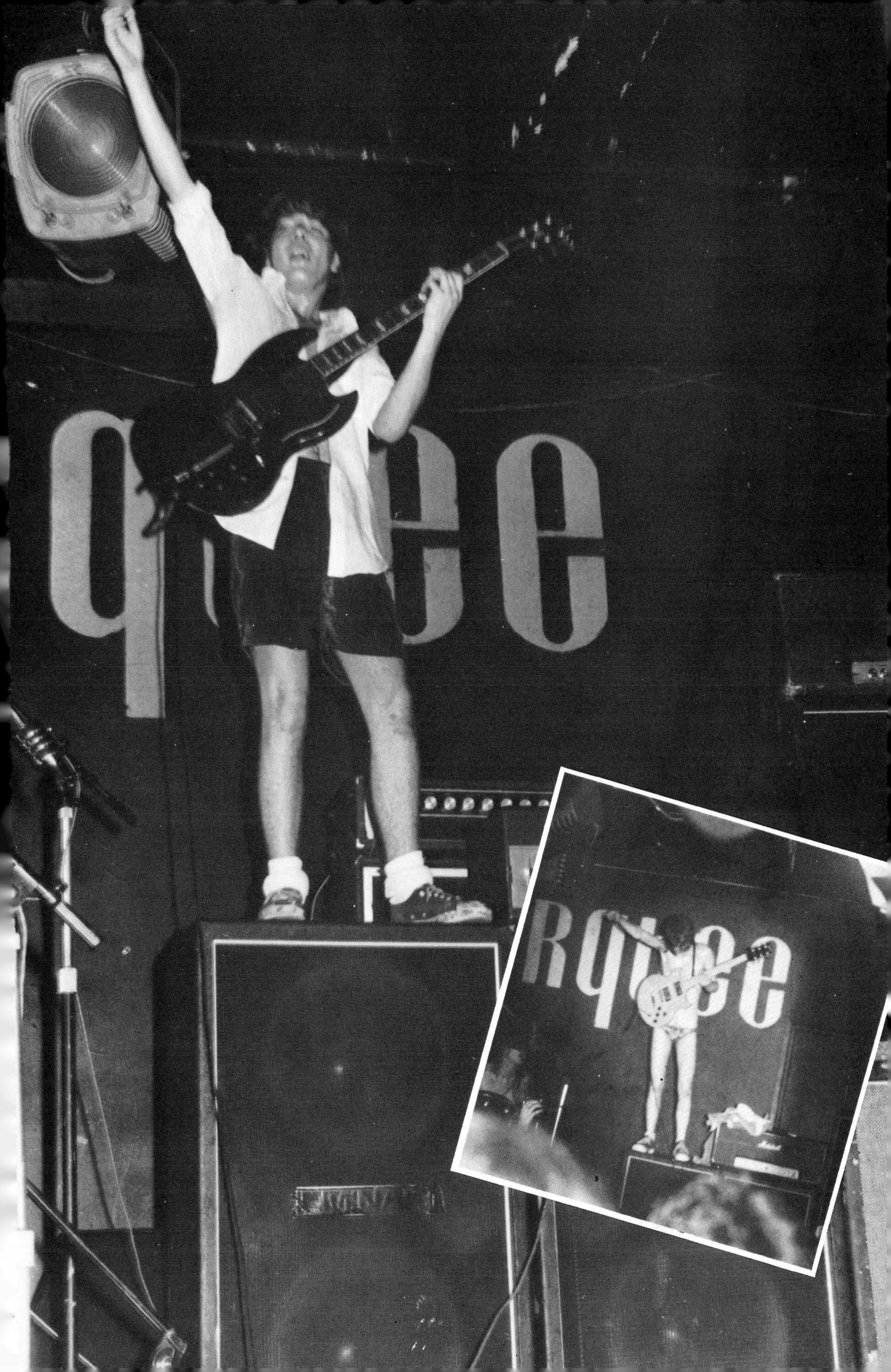

HIT DISC DIALS UP SEXY PHONE PESTS

A SET of vital statistics on a rock group's smash-hit record has landed them in an amazing £120,000 lawsuit.

For a couple claim the figures are the same as their phone number.

And as a result, they've had hundreds of obscene calls from the heavy-breathing brigade.

But last night, the top rock band AC-DC hit back: "It's just an innocent coincidence."

Their record — Dirty Deeds Done Dirt Cheap —is about sex-obsessed telephone pests.

But lead guitarist Angus Young, 24, who wrote the lyrics, said: "The numbers don't refer to any particular telephone. They are simply my dream girl's vital statistics—36-24-36.

"I thought any red-blooded male would realise that."

Norman and Marilyn White, though, whose phone number in Liberty-ville, Illinois, is 362-436, claim "considerable distress" from dirty callers since the disc was released in the States.

And through lawyers, they are demanding that the group withdraw the record for the words to be re-written.

Defending

They are also claiming 250,000 dollars compensation.

A spokesman for AC-DC's London agents said last night: "We're defending this to the hilt.

"We can't see why the Whites don't just change their number if they are so upset.

"But obviously they seem to think lawsuits are more entertaining over there."

It is the eternal rebellion

Rebellion because if you have said you are going to live honestly, then you have to put down what you see as being dishonest (and this covers pretentious or precious attitudes, as well as any kind of bullshit). Rebellion through Rock'n'Roll—against all kinds of societal impositions and restraints, from religion to sex—has always made sense to kids and grown-up young-at-hearts. It is the eternal rebellion, and one which AC/DC have to use. It is the only way they can relate or be related to.

Escape from responsibility (if only in a temporary way, to wind down and get refreshed), from intolerable living conditions, and from insincerity.

AC/DC don't admit to being rebellious. I don't know why. Perhaps they think 'rebellion' is too serious a word. They prefer to say they are having 'fun'. But 'fun' bands are ten-a-penny, and 'fun' by itself is too innocuous a word to describe AC/DC. If they were just a 'fun' band they would not be Rock'n'Roll.

Brian: ''We're just pranksters more than anything. You're having fun and that's all there is. If a kid thinks he's being naughty by singing *Highway To Hell, great,* because all he's doing is singing or chanting or putting his arms in the air. It's not meant to harm anyone. It's not like I'm coming out with my personal views and this individual meaning to life. If you do that you're in the same baseball game as those religious fanatics, or those English bands who hop on a cause, any cause, just to get themselves a bit of publicity.''

No, I think AC/DC *is* coming out with personal views, which the band express in their music, otherwise the music would have no power. To be fair to Brian, he is here defending his music against moral attack, and so he is probably overstressing the innocence angle. But the band's moral critics would not bother attacking the music if it were inocuous, and so I cannot agree that the band is fun per se.

AC/DC music is *fun because* it is rebellious (and honest, and an escape valve). But this doesn't mean either that the band incite mobs to rush out and do all the things *Highway To Hell* suggests. Their music is making a point, while having fun, and no one but a nuttola is going to think that the music is saying anything else. If we take any other view (i.e.) the pure fun one, it is to say that the band's lyrics are not seriously intended. Did Bon Scott, and millions of other kids world-wide who related to his life, not seriously mean what he wrote? I don't think so— just as I don't think that the rebellions against society shown by the band in their private lives are not the driving force behind their music.

"Chuck Berry was put in prison"

AC/DC would have us think their name is innocent. 'Found', Angus claims on the back of a sister-in-law's sewing machine, the letters are the abbreviations, in electrical terminology, of 'Alternating Current' and 'Direct Current', and *don't* represent the London/New York slang meaning of bisexuality. Well, that could be true, I suppose, and possibly AC/DC didn't intend their name to have value in that sense. When the name was thought up they were, after all, schoolkids living in a relatively naive culture. But 1973 when the band started, was not a particularly naive year. The term 'AC/DC' was legitimate in the San Francisco gay community at least as early as the mid-60s. And in London, at the end of the 60s, progressive theater had been turned upsidedown by the performance of a play by a young, new playwright, Heathcote Williams. (Williams has since risen to notoriety on a number of fronts—among them star of Derek Jarman's

film *The Tempest,* and as lyricist for the anarchistic SID DID IT by Nazis Against Fascism; as a lyricist he has also been largely instrumental in the return to critical acclaim of Marianne Faithfull—he wrote *Why D'Ya Do It* on her BROKEN ENGLISH album; and last, but certainly not least, together with J.G. Ballard, he is probably England's best living writing stylist.) The title of Williams' play was AC/DC, and in it he specifically set out to question sexual attitudes. Since that date no British Rockstar-to-be would have been unaware of the street meaning of 'AC/DC'.

If the meaning of 'AC/DC' is not intended to fun-shock most other aspects about the band certainly are. As Brian says: ''Chuck Berry was put in prison more times than too much, sometimes because of his color, or because of the tax, but mainly, I think, because he played the 'Devil's music'. We know that AC/DC are one of the biggest threats to Christianity in the world at the moment, for the same reason.''

Their lyrics are drawn from experience—on the road, back home in Australia, screwing, feeling the power of the crowd. They are honest, and, most of them, for me at least, reflect a rebellious attitude—in their content, in their musical expression and in the way they are performed on stage—although Angus plays down the dark side of AC/DC and tries to make it all sound like a harmless picnic. If you disagree with me, read Robert Palmer's *Jerry Lee Lewis Rocks!* (Omnibus Press). Palmer kicks the living shit out of the put down that Rock'n'Roll is harmless fun, and he does it a lot better than I!

Heathcote Williams author of "AC/DC", 1982.

——CHAPTER THIRTEEN——

When Led Zeppelin elected to step down at the end of 1981, in theory they made room at the top for another 'world leader'. But there was no one who could fill that place, and I doubt whether any Heavy Rock band ever again will occupy such a prestigious position. Zeppelin were the first of their kind, and nowadays there are too many bands competing for a share of the market for history to crystallize out in the same way. Nevertheless, if there is one band who could conceivably qualify for the hypothetical position, it must be AC/DC.

In 1982 the band are dominant figures who, unlike other bands (who have built up powerful *local* followings, e.g., Motorhead in Britain, Journey and Foreigner in the States) have attracted broad, general world-wide appeal. Motorhead are a good band who may have a stronger following in Britain right now than AC/DC, but their music is too bleak and harsh for general tastes in the States; Journey and Foreigner might find masses of juice-heads in their home country and Australia, but they won't find so many among the less sophisticated, brasher British kids.

AC/DC music hits right down the middle, excessive but restrained, brash but mature. The band rely on themselves and the timeless human escapes of having fun in the conventional sense, and their music is totally unsupported by off-putting props (the Nazi fetishism of Judas Priest, the fantasy imagery of Gillan and Iron Maiden). But for all that, it is not bland; it retains the juvenile power and rebellion that other bands can muster yet makes it acceptable to ordinary nostalgic older people trapped in responsible situations, as well as to the kids.

Yet what will the future hold? The band have already given fans many classic and memorable numbers—*Bad Boy Boogie, She's Got The Jack, Live Wire, Whole Lotta Rosie, Problem Child, Hells Bells, Sin City, Back In Black, Rock'n'Roll, Ain't Noise Pollution, Let's Get It Up*—and there will be more where they came from.

I also think that the band will continue to gather audience, and will become increasingly heavyweight and become more of an immovable fixture like Led Zeppelin became. With BACK IN BLACK, I think AC/DC gave birth to a new lease of their life, and if that is so they still have a *long* way to go. And I also think that within a few years they will have to 'modify' their sound yet again, or else (like the Stones) tour less frequently, because that youthful energy required for present sets will not last as long as their audience, and some way will have to be found of moderating the damage to young Angus' 'ead!

But that is jumping up front a bit.

Angus: "I don't think I would ever trade me life, 'cause I enjoyed the actual playing from the start; that's what I liked most of all. And the recording, being able to *make* music and knowing how it was done, that's what I liked, instead of having to sit down and listen to someone else doing it. You have so much more fun doing it yourself 'cause you're part of it.

"I've had a lot of bumps and ups and downs along the way, but I wouldn't change things—in fact, the only thing that disappoints me is the *bullshit* that a lot of people come out with. You get all these crap people, the ones who want to know you now who didn't want to know you before—all that shit.

"Suddenly, these people start saying how much they appreciate something they really hate and would rather be at home watching TV instead of hearing. The ones that I really hate are those who walk in now and say it's the first time they've ever seen us and what a great show it is, but where were they five years ago when we started up?

"I had that with this DJ who came into our dressing room recently and said, 'Hi, I'm so-and-so from so-and-so, I used to listen to your albums a few years ago and, to be honest with you, I didn't like them, but these kids kept ringing up and requesting them and gradually I've grown to like it'.

"And I just said to him, 'Pal, with us you either like it or hate it and if you didn't like it then I'll be buggered if you like it now'. I just told him what I thought and showed him the door.

"I remember he came out with some other stupid things like how he couldn't understand the singer's words! I mean, the guy's not singing, he's yelling his guts out. Who sings in a real rock band? They should save all that for Barely Manenough (Barry Manilow—geddit?), not us."

90

DISCOGRAPHY

ALBUMS

High Voltage
(ALBERT PRODUCTIONS APLP 009)
A. Baby Please Don't Go (Broonzy)
   She's Got Balls (Young/Young/Scott)
   Little Lover (Young/Young/Scott)
   Stick Around (Young/Young/Scott)
B. Soul Stripper (Young/Young)
   You Ain't Got A Hold On Me
   (Young/Young/Scott)
   Love Song (Young/Young/Scott)
   Show Business (Young/Young/Scott)
Produced by Vanda & Young

TNT (ALBERT RECORDS APLP 0016)
A. It's A Long Way To The Top (If You Wanna
   Rock'n'Roll) (Young/Young/Scott)
   The Rock'n'Roll Singer
   (Young/Young/Scott)
   She's Got The Jack (Young/Young/Scott)
   Live Wire (Young/Young/Scott)
B. TNT (Young/Young/Scott)
   Rocker (Young/Young/Scott)
   Can I Sit Next To You Girl (Young/Young)
   High Voltage (Young/Young/Scott)
   School Days (Perry)
Produced by Vanda & Young

High Voltage
(ATLANTIC K5027; CAS.K450257.
Released 14 May 1976)
A. It's A Long Way To The Top
   Rock'n'Roll Singer
   She's Got The Jack
   Live Wire
   TNT
B. Can I Sit Next To You Girl
   Little Lover
   She's Got Balls
   High Voltage
All tracks taken from **High Voltage** and **TNT**
'Albert Productions' albums.
Produced by Vanda & Young.

Dirty Deeds Done Dirt Cheap
(ATLANTIC K50323, CAS.K450323.
Released 17 December 1976)
A. Dirty Deeds Done Dirt Cheap
   Love At First Feel
   Big Balls
   Rocker
   Problem Child
B. There's Gonna Be Some Rockin'
   Ain't No Fun Waitin' To Be A Millionaire
   Ride On
   Squealer
All titles by Young/Young/Scott.
Produced by Vanda & Young.

Let There Be Rock
(ATLANTIC K50366, CAS.K450366.
Released 14 October 1977)
A. Go Down
   Dog Eat Dog
   Let There Be Rock
   Bad Boy Boogie
B. Overdose
   Crabsody In Blue
   Hell Ain't A Bad Place To Be
   Whole Lotta Rosie
All titles by Young/Young/Scott.
Produced by Vanda & Young.

Powerage (ATLANTIC K50483, CAS.K450483.
Released 28 April 1978)
A. Gimme A Bullet
   Down Payment Blues
   Gone Shootin'
   Riff Raff
B. Sin City
   Up To My Neck In You
   What's Next To The Moon
   Cold Hearted Man
   Kicked In The Teeth
All titles by Young/Young/Scott.
Produced by Vanda & Young.

If You Want Blood You've Got It
(ATLANTIC K50532, CAS.K450532.
Released 13 October 1978)
A. Riff Raff
   Hell Ain't A Bad Place To Be
   Bad Boy Boogie
   The Jack
   Problem Child
B. Whole Lotta Rosie
   Rock'n'Roll Damnation
   High Voltage
   Let There Be Rock
   Rocker
Live album. Produced by Vanda & Young.

Highway To Hell
(ATLANTIC K50628, CAS.K450628.
Released 27 July 1979)
A. Highway To Hell
   Girls Got Rhythm
   Walk All Over You
   Touch Too Much
   Beating Around The Bush
B. Shot Down In Flames
   Get It Hot
   If You Want Blood (You've Got It)
   Love Hungry Man
   Night Prowler
Produced by Robert John Lange.

Back In Black (ATLANTIC K50737.
Released 31 July 1980)
A. Hells Bells
   Shoot To Thrill
   What Do You Do For Money Honey
   Give The Dog A Bone
   Let Me Put My Love Into You
B. Back In Black
   You Shook Me All Night Long
   Have A Drink On Me
   Shake A Leg
   Rock And Roll Ain't Noise Pollution
All tracks Young/Young/Johnson.
Produced by Robert John Lange.

For Those About To Rock (We Salute You)
(ATLANTIC K50851. Released November 1981)
A. For Those About To Rock (We Salute You)
   Evil Walks
   C.O.D.
   Spell Bound
   Put The Finger On You

B. Let's Get It Up
   Inject The Venom
   Breaking The Rules
   Snowballed
   Night Of The Long Knives
All tracks by Young/Young/Johnson.
Produced by Robert John Lange.

Boxed Set (ATLANTIC 31146.
French import only)
High Voltage (Album)
Dirty Deeds Done Dirt Cheap (Album)
Powerage (Album)
Baby Please Don't Go (EP, also including **Soul Stripper** and **Jailbreak**)

Boxed Set (ALBERT PRODUCTIONS.
Title: **AC/DC**. Australian import)
Highway To Hell (Album)
Powerage (Album)
TNT (Album)
Dirty Deeds Done Dirt Cheap (Album)
Let There Be Rock (Album)
High Voltage (Album)
Cold Hearted Man (12″ 45. No reverse side.
Available only with this boxed set)
All albums in original sleeves; special sleeve on
the 12″. Includes iron-on transfer of AC/DC
logo. Package is grey box with flaming AC/DC
logo on the front, album and track listing on
the back.

SINGLES

Jailbreak/Fling Thing (ATLANTIC K108508.
Released January 1976)*
**It's A Long Way To The Top If You Wanna
Rock'n'Roll/Can I Sit Next To You Girl**
(ATLANTIC K10745. Released April 1976)
High Voltage/Live Wire
(ATLANTIC K10860.
Released 29 October 1976)
**Dirty Deeds Done Dirt Cheap/Big Balls/The
Jack** (Maxi Record. ATLANTIC K10899.
Released January 1977)
Big Balls/The Jack
(ATLANTIC K50323, K50257. Released 1976)
Let There Be Rock/Problem Child
(ATLANTIC K11018.
Released 30 September 1977)
Rock'n'Roll Damnation/Sin City
(ATLANTIC K11142. Released 26 May 1978)

Whole Lotta Rosie/Hell Ain't A Bad Place To Be (ATLANTIC K11207.
Released 27 October 1978)
Highway To Hell/If You Want Blood
(ATLANTIC K11207. Released 3 August 1979)
Girls Got Rhythm/Get It Hot (ATLANTIC
K11406. Released 9 November 1979)
**Girls Got Rhythm/If You Want Blood/Hell
Ain't A Bad Place To Be/Rock'n'Roll
Damnation** (ATLANTIC K11406E. Extended
play. Released 9 November 1979)
**Touch Too Much/Live Wire/Shot Down In
Flames** (ATLANTIC K11435.
Released 25 January 1980)
High Voltage/Live Wire (ATLANTIC HM1.
Re-issue. Released 28 June 1980)
**Dirty Deeds Done Dirt Cheap/Big Balls/
The Jack** (ATLANTIC HM2.
Released 28 June 1980)
**It's A Long Way To The Top/Can I Sit Next To
You Girl** (ATLANTIC HM3. Re-issue.
Released 28 June 1980)
**Whole Lotta Rosie/Hell Ain't A Bad Place To
Be** (ATLANTIC HM4. Re-issue.
Released 28 June 1980)
**You Shook Me All Night Long/Have A Drink
On Me** (ATLANTIC K11600. Re-issue.
Released 5 September 1980)
**Rock'n'Roll Ain't Noise Pollution/Have
A Drink On Me** (ATLANTIC K11630T.
Released 21 November 1980)
Let's Get It Up/TNT (Live) (ATLANTIC
K11706. Released January 1982)
**Let's Get It Up/TNT (Live)/Back In Black
(Live)** (12'' single. ATLANTIC K11706T.
Released January 1982).

Albums featuring Cliff Williams (With 'Home')
Pause For A Hoarse Horse (EPIC EPC 64365.
Released 1970)
Home (CBS 64752. Released 1971)
The Alchemist (CBS 65550. Released 1972)
(With 'Bandit')
Bandit (ARISTA ARTY 148. Released 1977)

Albums featuring Brian Johnson
(With 'Geordie')
Hope You Like It (EMI EMC3001.
Released 1973)
Master Of Rock (EMI 054 95689. Released 1974)
Don't Be Fooled By The Name (EMA 764.
Released 1974)
Save The World (EMI EMC 3134.
Released 1976)
Geordie (Featuring Brian Johnson. RED BUS
RBMP 5001. Released December 1980)

BOOTLEGS

AC/DC, Featuring Bon Scott—Live In Germany
A. Live Wire
   Sin City
   Walk Over You
   Girls Got The Rhythm
   T.N.T.
B. Highway
   High Voltage
   Whole Lotta Rosie
   Rocker
Manufactured in France. Deluxe black and white
cover.

110/220 (IMPOSSIBLE RECORDWORKS 1-31)
A. Live Wire
   Problem Child
   High Voltage
   Hell Ain't A Bad Place To Be
B. Dog Eat Dog
   The Jack
   Whole Lotta Rosie
   Rocker
Album is of excellent stereo quality. Source:
Atlantic Studios, New York City, Dec. 7 1977.
Deluxe black and white cover.

AC/DC, Bon Scott's Last Oui Oui
(DRIVILE RECORDS DCP600)
A. Live Wire
   Hell Ain't A Bad Place To Be
   Sin City
B. Walk All Over You
   Bad Boy Boogie
C. The Jack
   Highway To Hell
   High Voltage
D. Whole Lotta Rosie
   Rocker
   TNT
Album is of excellent stereo quality, recorded in
Paris 12/9/79. Deluxe color cover.

AC/DC,—Electric Shock (WL-9)
A. Live Wire
   Long Way To The Top
   Soul Stripper
   High Voltage

B. Baby Please Don't Go
   Let There Be Rock
   Problem Child
   Hell Ain't A Bad Place To Be
C. Bad Boy Boogie
   I'm A Rocker
   Whole Lotta Rosie
   Rocker
D. If You Want Blood
   Let There Be Rock
   The Jack
   Highway To Hell
Album is excellent stereo (Side A has hiss); Side D
good and very good stereo. Tracks 1-5 'In
Concert', London Jan/'76; tracks 6-10 London
Mar/'77; tracks 11-16 Rockville, Md., Oct/'79.
Deluxe color cover.

AC/DC—Live (1812)
A. Hells Bells
   Bad Boy Boogie
   The Jack
B. Highway To Hell
   High Voltage
   You Shook Me All Night Long
   Let There Be Rock
Album is excellent mono. European bootleg with
deluxe b&w cover and song separation.

AC/DC—Live '76
A. It's A Long Way To The Top
   Soul Stripper
   Baby Please Don't Go
   Little Lover
B. Can I Sit Next To You Girl
   Live Wire
   Jailbreak
   The Rock'n'Roll Singer
   Schooldays
Tracks 1-3 'In Concert' BBC London (excellent
mono); tracks 4-6 'In Concert' BBC sessions,
London (excellent stereo); track 7, Marc Bolan
TV Show 28/8/76 (excellent mono); tracks 8&9,
Reading Festival, Reading, England, 29/8/76
(very good stereo). Swedish bootleg on red vinyl;
only 650 made. Song separation. White jacket
with title embossed in black.

AC/DC—Live '77
A. Let There Be Rock
   Rocker
   She's Got Balls
   TNT

B. Up To My Neck In You
   Kicked In The Teeth
   The Jack

Track 2, BBC 'In Concert', London, October;
track 3, Offenbach, W. Germany, April 29, very
good mono; track 4, Mayfair, Newcastle,
October 14, very good mono; track 7, Old
Waldorf, San Francisco, September 1. Recording
is excellent stereo. Number 2 in the 'Swedish
series' (see **AC/DC—Live '76,** above; same
specifications apply).

AC/DC—Live '78
A. Live Wire
   Problem Child
   Gone Shooting
   Bad Boy Boogie
B. Rock'n'Roll Damnation
   Down Payment Blues
   Fling Thing
   Rocker
   Dog Eat Dog
Track 4, Paradise Theater, Boston, October 21;
track 5, Nijmegen, Holland, October 23; track 6,
Glasgow, April 30, excellent mono; track 8,
Boston, October 21. Recording is excellent stereo.
Number 3 in the 'Swedish series' (see **AC/DC—
Live '76,** above; same specifications apply).

AC/DC—Live '79
A. Bad Boy Boogie
   The Jack
   Highway To Hell
   If You Want Blood
B. Shot Down In Flames
   Sin City
   Walk All Over You
   Girls Got Rhythm
   TNT
   Let There Be Rock
Excellent stereo. Tracks 1-5, Towson, Md.,
October 16; tracks 6-10, Paris, December 9,
evening show. Number 4 in the 'Swedish series'
(see **AC/DC—Live '76,** above; same
specifications apply).

BOOTLEG VIDEOS

AC/DC—Live, Countdown Holland. 1980.
Color. 25 minutes.
AC/DC—Live at Essex University (UK). Color
(flicks to b/w towards end). 40 minutes.